Dr. John Porter used to teach geography at a sixth form college in Hampshire but has always had a strong interest in the history of Dorset and the Wessex region. Since coming to live in Gillingham he has been able to give time to research and writing. He lectures regularly for the Workers Educational Association in Dorset, Somerset and Wiltshire.

Following page

Wyke Regis's expansion from a small downland village into what is effectively a suburb of Weymouth began with the opening of the huge factory of the Whitehead Torpedo Company at Ferry Bridge in 1891. After the Second World War new housing estates were built between Wyke Regis, Portland Harbour and the Rodwell area of Weymouth, and in recent years the site of the torpedo factory has also been developed. But as this view of the allotments at Wyke Regis shows, Dorset's towns still retain their ancient links with the surrounding countryside.

TOWNS

JOHN PORTER

THE DOVECOTE PRESS

Wareham, with the old bridge over the River Frome and Lady St
Mary Church before the replacement of the Saxon nave in 1841.
To the left of the bridge was originally Abbot's Quay, but by the
date of this engraving the quay had been built over and is here
shown occupied by tenements.

First published in 2008 by The Dovecote Press Ltd
Stanbridge, Wimborne Minster, Dorset BH21 4JD

ISBN 978 1 904 34956 3

Typeset in Monotype Sabon
Printed and bound by Baskerville Press, Salisbury, Wiltshire

A CIP catalogue record for this book is available
from the British Library

CONTENTS

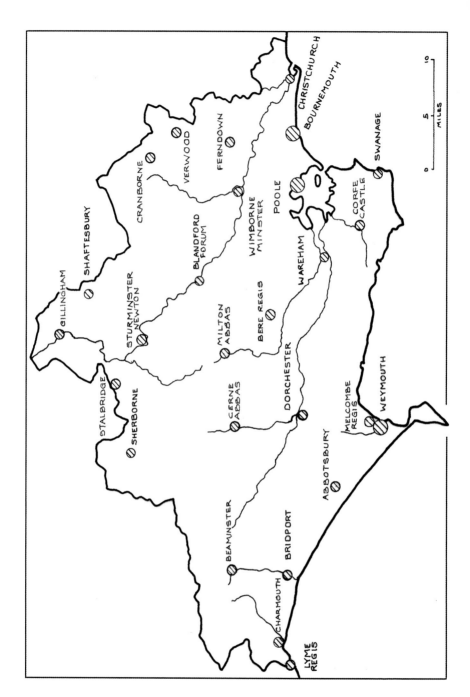

THE ORIGINS OF DORSET'S TOWNS

There are over twenty places in Dorset which have the status of towns, or were once considered to be towns in the past. Some of these, notably Bournemouth and Poole, are today part of the urban sprawl which stretches from southern Hampshire almost into Purbeck. Others, such as Beaminster or Shaftesbury, once depended on their flourishing markets, and today still provide important services for the surrounding countryside. There are also smaller places which were once thought of as towns, but never grew much beyond the size of large villages.

There is no evidence of town life in Dorset, in the way in which we would understand the term, during prehistoric times. At Hengistbury Head a large trading settlement developed in the late Iron Age, around 100 BC, with continental wine and luxury goods being imported in return for exports of iron ore, minerals, and grain. Although this site may have been well used by traders, there is nothing to show that it grew into a town. Further trade may have been centred on the larger hillforts, such as Maiden Castle, which besides being defensive acted as tribal and administrative centres, and so would also have attracted exchange and commerce. But none of the hillforts later grew into towns.

The Roman occupation brought a period of peace and stability to Dorset, resulting in population growth and a flourishing countryside of prosperous villas and farms. After subduing the Iron Age defenders of Maiden Castle the Romans built a fort nearby to control the area. This was later superseded by the new Roman town of Durnovaria, or Roman Dorchester, around 70 AD. The new town later acquired a wide ditch and earthen bank for defences, and sometime after 300 AD the earthen rampart was faced with a stone wall. The alignment of the walls, which enclose an area of some 33 hectares, largely determined the extent of the later town until the nineteenth century, even though

Dorchester was called *Durnovaria* by the Romans and was Dorset's first proper town. It had walls, gates, public buildings, heated baths, an amphitheatre, and its own water supply. The best surviving evidence of the sophistication of Roman urban life is the well-preserved town house behind County Hall in Colliton Street.

the walls themselves eventually disappeared. The position of the old Roman walls today is represented in the South and West Walks, one of the town's most attractive features.

Within the walls are features which suggest the former importance of Roman Dorchester. High East and High West Streets follow the alignment of the Roman road through the town, and there would have been gates at either end where the it passed through the walls. A further gate stood at the southern end of South Street. Enough is known of the Roman street plan to indicate that it would have been a grid pattern. The mosaic floors of some houses have come to light, and the remains of a Roman town house, sometimes considered the best example of its kind in Britain, can be seen in Colliton Park near the County Hall. Outside the walls, south of the town, the Neolithic henge monument of Maumbury Rings was made into an amphitheatre, used during the first and second centuries. Perhaps the most remarkable structure of Roman times was the aqueduct which brought water to the town for public baths and domestic use from the River Frome near Frampton; parts of its course can still be traced along the hillside above the river.

There is no indication that the flourishing urban life of Dorchester continued after the departure of the Romans early in the fifth century. The Romanised population of the region was gradually subordinated to waves of Saxon settlers from the east. The contents of seventh century Saxon graves are typically those of families rather than warriors, suggesting that permanent settlement was taking place. In the ninth century the Saxons were themselves beset by invasions of Vikings. Throughout this period the population throughout Dorset appears to have been dispersed in small settlements, and there is no evidence of larger places which might be regarded as towns.

However some settlements were clearly more important than others, and this was particularly true of places associated with the early church. The Saxon conquests were soon followed by the establishment of a monastery and bishop's see at Sherborne, with Aldhelm as the first bishop (705). Some consider that this Saxon

J.H.P. Gibb's reconstruction of the Saxon cathedral in Sherborne. A monastery and the bishop's see were established in 705, with Aldhelm as first bishop and a diocese that included Dorset, Somerset and part of Wiltshire.

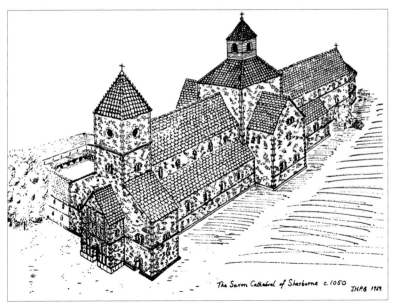

church succeeded another, earlier Celtic church known to historians as Lanprobus. About the same time a monastery was founded at Wimborne by Cuthburga, sister of the West Saxon King Ine, and Wareham also had a Saxon nunnery. All three places show evidence that Romano-British peoples had lived nearby, but there is no likelihood that they were towns at that time. In the Saxon period they were not much more than large villages clustered around the monasteries.

Other places of importance in Saxon Dorset include those with 'minster' names, such as Sturminster, Yetminster, and Charminster. A minster was a community of priests, smaller than that of a monastery, whose task was to care for the spiritual life of the population of the region around them. Minsters, which had large territories or 'parochia', are considered to be the 'mother' churches of parishes which developed later. Other places, such as Twinham (Christchurch) were also minsters, despite not having this in their name. The territories of minsters have been shown to correspond to those of royal manors or estates, suggesting that royal authority or patronage may have been important in their creation.

The minster at Wimborne was based on a 'double monastery' of monks and nuns. The two monasteries, although both ruled by the abbess, were kept separate, an early description telling us that 'two monasteries were of old founded by kings . . . surrounded with high and stout walls'. This important site was destroyed by the Danes in the tenth century, but was succeeded by a college of secular canons built by Edward the Confessor. The college buildings may have been to the south of the minster church, perhaps in the area of the later grammar school. By the eleventh century a town large enough to be regarded as a borough had grown up around the minster and college.

Other minster places which were still small at this time proved important enough to grow into towns at a later date, such as Sturminster (Newton), already a royal estate and minster by the ninth century. In 968 King Edgar gave the manor to Glastonbury Abbey, and it is likely that from this time the 'new' 'tun' or settlement across the River Stour can be dated, for it was here that the Abbot of Glastonbury built a manor house inside the ramparts of an old Iron Age hillfort.

The reign of King Alfred (871-899) marked a major step in the development of towns in Dorset and neighbouring parts of Wessex. The Danish invasions of the late ninth century convinced Alfred of the need for a defensive system for his Wessex kingdom. This was the origin of the towns known as burhs, a word which later came to mean boroughs. The burhs were a series of fortified towns, and their names are recorded in the document known as the Burghal Hidage. Many of them were around the periphery of the kingdom and along the coast, where they were best placed to repel invaders, but some occupied strategic points inland. The Dorset burhs were Christchurch, Wareham, Bridport, and Shaftesbury. In Somerset there were burhs at Langport and Axbridge, in Wiltshire at Malmesbury, Wilton, Chisbury, and Cricklade, and in Hampshire at Winchester, Portchester, and at Southampton.

Wareham preserves something of the feel of a Saxon burh even today. A preliminary walk around the town, with its pleasant eighteenth-century shops and houses, suggests the Georgian period. However Wareham's fabric disguises much earlier origins. The old part occupies a defensive position on a ridge between the rivers Piddle and Frome, making it a natural choice for a burh. The Saxon burh is surrounded by the remains of a three-sided system of ditch and bank fortifications, which still form a striking perimeter to the old town. Within this enclosed space of some 40 hectares the streets form a planned grid-iron pattern which has remained little disturbed since Saxon times. The long straight streets enabled defenders to reach the walls quickly in event of an attack. The landed wealth of the town was assessed at 1,600 hides, and it has been calculated that this would have been enough to provide the manpower needed for the town's defence.

Wareham's Quay is a reminder of its role as a major Saxon river port, a position which it eventually lost to Poole in later centuries. Wareham also has two churches associated with its Saxon past: St. Martin's, on the east side of the gateway to the town, preserves its

The Norman Bargate in Christchurch, demolished in 1744. It stood north of the roundabout at the junction of the by-pass and High Street. The room over the gate was probably either a chapel or the town lock-up.

Saxon architecture of the eleventh century; but it is predated by the church of Lady St. Mary on The Green, a nineteenth century building on the site of an eighth century minster church. When Lady St. Mary's was being rebuilt, five stones with Celtic inscriptions were discovered; a direct link between the Saxon town and an even earlier past.

Other defensive strong points in south Dorset were Christchurch and Bridport. Christchurch lies between the rivers Stour and Avon at the end of a low promontory of river gravels, and commands the safe anchorage of Christchurch Harbour. The finding of an early Saxon cemetery to the north of the town suggests that there may have been a Saxon settlement here well before Alfred's time. Like Wareham, the town was protected by a defensive bank and ditch, but only on its northern and western sides; the southern and eastern sides were defended by marshes. The defences seem to have been made of earth, rubble, and turf, with a ditch on the outside and a palisade fence on the top. The main street, now the High Street, ran along the top of the ridge, with a northern gate on the line of the defensive bank, later succeeded by the Norman gate of Bargate. Although Christchurch was of strategic importance it may have been less successful economically, and failed to grow into a town until later.

The name Bridport means port (market town) belonging to Bredy, a hillfort site 8 miles to the east. Bridport appears in the Burghal Hidage as Brydian, and there has always been some uncertainty as to whether this name refers to the present Bridport or to the hillfort settlement which was deserted for the present site sometime before the Conquest. Saxon Bridport was similar to Wareham and Christchurch in occupying a promontory position between rivers. But unlike them it was too far from the sea to have its own quays, and for centuries had to depend on goods being ferried to larger vessels anchored at the mouth of the River Brit. The Saxon town can be recognised today along the length of South Street, where there would have been a wide market space between the rows of houses on either side. Property boundary lines between these houses may well reflect Saxon boundaries,

Bridport in 1774, showing the long narrow plots behind the houses lining South Street which were to become rope walks.

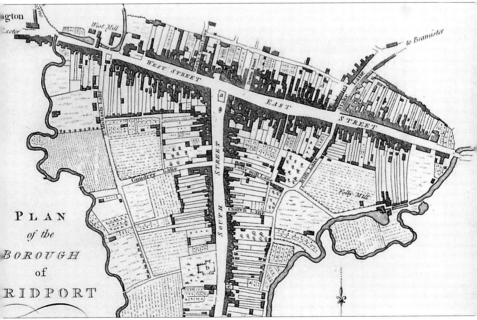

while the long 'burgage' plots extending backwards from the street were of immense value to the later rope industry. From a combination of archaeological and documentary research it is possible to suggest the position of the defensive town ditches, which may have been more prominent along the eastern side of the town.

In the north of the county, Shaftesbury was a major strategic point, its dramatic and exposed 220 metre high hilltop site controlling routes down the north-south Great Ridgeway and the route from London to the west country. Ninth-century Shaftesbury seems to have been an entirely new settlement. Its spectacular natural defensive position can be readily appreciated from a walk along the spur by the side of the old abbey precinct. The steep sides of the promontory provided natural ramparts, with no need for defensive banks and ditches, except across the neck of the spur. Alfred followed the establishment of the burh with the founding of Shaftesbury Abbey, a Benedictine nunnery, although some documents suggest that an earlier foundation may already have existed. The Abbey became especially well known as a centre for pilgrimage after the burial there of King Edward the Martyr in 979. Today the ruins fail to convey the extent of the former abbey with its various monastery buildings, which spread across much of the promontory, but the impressive precinct wall on Gold Hill is a reminder of its domination of the town until 1539.

Some places did not become burhs but were important for other reasons. Despite becoming the new episcopal see for the western part of Wessex, Sherborne failed to develop further, and this may have been a reason why the bishopric was eventually moved to Old Sarum in 1075. Dorchester, where urban life had collapsed after the end of the Roman period, became a royal estate, and the royal residence was an important enough place for charters to be signed by visiting kings. In 789 the invading Danes were met by the king's reeve riding out from Dorchester. He probably thought they were traders, but unfortunately paid for this mistake with his life. Dorchester became a market and a mint in the reign of Athelstan (925-939), and by late Saxon times it had given its name to the shire: 'Dorset: the people dependent on Dorchester'.

Part of an alabaster altar piece from Shaftesbury Abbey depicting the reburial of St Edward the Martyr in the Abbey. The young King Edward was murdered by his stepmother whilst hunting in Purbeck in 979 and temporarily buried in Wareham.

THE TOWNS IN DOMESDAY BOOK

Domesday Book gives us a more detailed glimpse of how far Dorset's towns had developed by the end of the Saxon period. The survey, a record of landholding and estates, was made in 1086, twenty years after the Conquest, and also compares the wealth of estates at that time with what they had been worth in 1066 at the end of the reign of Edward the Confessor.

The only four places named as 'boroughs' were Bridport, Dorchester, Shaftesbury, and Wareham. Shaftesbury was the largest, with 257 households in 1066 belonging to the king and the abbess, suggesting a population of around 1,300. However the estimation of population sizes from Domesday Book is always problematical, and the true population may have been larger. A measure of the importance of all these places is the recording of moneyers, of which Shaftesbury had three, indicating the existence of mints. All four towns had suffered badly from the devastation wrought by William the Conqueror's army in the years following the Conquest. On the king's estate in Wareham there had been 143 households in 1066, but only 70 remained at the time of the survey in 1086.

Domesday Book also refers to places which, although not described as boroughs, were nevertheless by 1086 taking on some of the characteristics of towns. Wimborne Minster is recorded as having burgesses, or leading citizens of boroughs, the existence of whom is often taken as a measure of urban status. Sherborne and Christchurch were smaller, perhaps still large villages clustered around the religious houses. Gillingham had a church and was a royal estate, and may have been more important at this time than surviving evidence suggests. Smaller settlements recorded which were to develop into towns in the coming centuries were Beaminster, Blandford Forum, Cerne Abbas, Charmouth, Cranborne, Lyme Regis, Milton Abbas, Stalbridge, and Sturminster Newton.

It is difficult to know what any of these places might have looked like at this time. Several had substantial stone churches, but most other buildings would have been of timber or wattle and daub. Exceptions in stone might have been the homes of the wealthy or the king or lord's representative. Excavations in Shaftesbury, Dorchester, and Wareham have produced pottery and other remains indicative of a growing urban centre by the end of the Saxon period, as well as trading links with the surrounding countryside.

MEDIEVAL MARKETS, BOROUGHS & PORTS

At the start of the Norman period no more than half a dozen places in Dorset were recognisable as towns. Several others recorded in Domesday Book were large villages, often clustered around 'minster' churches, but still without essential features of urban life. During the next two centuries some villages completed their transformation into towns, while other towns appeared where there had been no previous settlement of any sort. By 1300 there were over twenty towns in Dorset, spread across the county, and there were few places which found themselves more than a few miles from one of them.

Much of this was due to the Norman lords, both lay and ecclesiastical, developing the assets represented by their estates. Throughout Dorset, as elsewhere in England, the population was increasing, generating an increase in the demand for food and farm produce. Lords were eager to increase their incomes, particularly where people regularly congregated to trade and exchange. By setting up new markets, some of the proceeds could be tapped off in the form of tolls and taxes. To hold a market, a lord had to obtain a market charter from the Crown, or be able to show that markets had already been held there for some considerable time.

Dorset, with its diversity of landscapes and farming, producing a mix of corn, cattle, sheep, and wool, together with its many landowners and their estates, was fertile ground for the growth of new markets. Between the reigns of John (1199-1216) and Henry VI (1422-1471) market rights were recognised or granted by the Crown to no fewer than 56 places in Dorset. The market was granted for a specific day of the week, and alongside it there was often the granting of an annual fair, to be held on a specified day, normally a saint's day.

However a large number of the market grants proved to be unsuccessful, with the anticipated trade failing to materialise and the market rights eventually lapsing. Only 21 of the markets were still functioning by 1600; the casualties were mostly smaller settlements such as Tarrant Gunville, Powerstock, Ryme Intrinseca, and Kingston Russell, to which market rights were granted but little is heard about any further trade. For many larger places, market grants were an important step on the way to becoming towns, with a once weekly market proving inadequate for the trade generated. At Milton Abbas the original grant of a Thursday market in 1252 was supplemented by a further grant of a Monday market in 1280. Similarly the 1252 fair grant (15 August), was added to with a further fair on 28 July. For several towns the date of the granting of market rights was a milestone in their commercial history.

BOROUGHS, BURGAGES, AND 'NEW' TOWNS

By the thirteenth century more Dorset places were being recognised as boroughs, and are described as such in the records of taxation which lords and their manors paid to the Crown. Blandford acquired its market grant in 1217 and was first named as a borough in 1244. By 1288 it was being known as Blandford Forum, meaning 'market'.

Poole, Weymouth, Melcombe Regis, and Lyme Regis were also boroughs by the middle of the thirteenth century. Lyme became involved in a dispute with Bridport, which claimed that Lyme was holding markets not only on Mondays, the day granted in the charter, but on every day of the week, to the detriment of the Bridport markets. Bridport was also involved in a similar dispute with Charmouth. Such was the competition for trade between medieval market centres that only the most successful could survive.

Borough status was eagerly sought by all aspiring towns. Elevation to a borough meant that the townspeople were able to go about their business free of some or all of the feudal obligations which applied elsewhere. The principal townsmen, known as burgesses, held their land by burgage tenure. Instead of rendering feudal dues, they paid a fixed rent to the lord and had the freedom to sell, rent, or transfer their lands to others as they wished. Through their trade associations or guilds they often formed the governing body of the town. These conditions encouraged them to develop their trade, commerce and businesses. In his turn the lord guaranteed the town's privileges and undertook to protect its markets and trading. Bridport, for example, received its charter as a free borough in 1253. The town was governed by a council of twelve burgesses and the town officers included bailiffs, constables, and wardens.

Some lords went a step further, and decided that the best way to develop trade and commerce was to build a new town by the side of the old one. At Bridport, Sherborne, and Wimborne Minster 'new towns' were created alongside the older Saxon town. In this way the lords continued to gain feudal dues from the old town while benefiting from the rents that could be levied on the burgages of the new town. At Wimborne, where the town was largely divided between the manors of the Dean of the Minster and the Lord of Kingston Lacy (the Duke of Lancaster), both lords endeavoured to create rival new boroughs outside the existing market centre. But despite the Kingston Lacy venture becoming known as the 'Borough manor', a name which lives on in some of Wimborne's principal streets, the town never received a royal borough charter.

Corfe Castle was another product of medieval new town development. The site had been a royal estate since Saxon times, and the castle was first built around 1080, being subsequently enlarged during the following centuries, particularly in the reign of King John. The town grew beneath its walls, and the economic importance of the nearby quarries swelled the population further. Probably because it was a royal manor attached to the castle, Corfe was recognised as a borough, and may have had a mayor, coroner, and bailiff. But its economy remained based on servicing the castle and the local quarrying industry, and the town remained small and was described as 'decayed' in 1325.

Cranborne and Bere Regis also benefited by royal involvement. King John acquired Cranborne and its Chase through marriage and built a hunting lodge, whose core still survives within the present manor house. The town grew in importance as the administrative centre of the law of the Chase, and in some documents is referred to as a borough, although no charter survives. Bere Regis, located on the Bere Stream and at a meeting of heath, down, and woodland, was

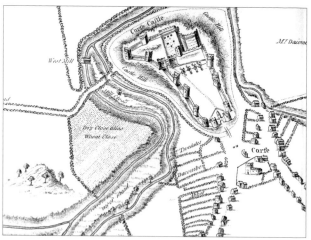

Corfe Castle in 1586, from Ralph Treswell's *Survey of Purbeck*. Corfe had been a Saxon royal estate, and the Castle was started after the Norman Conquest. Although a borough, and later a 'Rotten Borough' sending MPs to Parliament, the town of Corfe was no larger than many villages.

granted a market by John and owes its name to visits by him, but seems to have developed no further and has remained a large village into the present.

At Charmouth in 1320 the Abbot of Forde created a new free borough. The only constraints on burgesses were to use the abbot's mill and attend his court. Charmouth however was a 'late' new town, unable to compete with nearby established markets such as Lyme Regis, and remained dependent on the abbot's own estates. It appears to have grown little in the later medieval centuries, and is not represented on the taxation returns of 1332.

The least successful attempt to create a new town took place on an area of low-lying heathland overlooking Poole Harbour not far from Studland. Here in 1286 Edward I made a grant to the burgesses of Nova Villa ('new town'), but history records nothing further of the venture. The area around Newton Farm is considered to be the most likely site for the abortive town. The project came too late to be able to compete with the already established ports of Poole and Wareham, and is a reminder that in an age of competition for trade, only the strongest towns could survive.

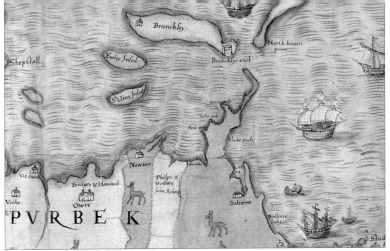

Another detail from the 1586 *Survey* shows Newton, of which only a farm bearing the name remains as evidence of Edward I's failed attempt to found a new town on the heathland overlooking Poole Harbour in 1286.

THE MEDIEVAL TOWNSCAPE

By the thirteenth century Dorset's towns presented a welcoming appearance to medieval travellers. The first glimpse would have been of a cluster of thatched rooftops, above which rose the imposing structure of an abbey or minster church. This would have been especially striking at Shaftesbury, where its many houses were clearly visible along the skyline, all grouped round the massive edifice of the abbey church. The first views of Christchurch from its harbour would

Shaftesbury in 1795, looking north towards Gold Hill, with the town's rooftops silhouetted against the skyline. The medieval town had 12 churches, 4 market crosses and two dozen inns.

Above The Square, Beaminster. The covered memorial of 1906 in the foreground marks the site of the market cross, demolished in about 1750. The only known description mentions 'a handsome Cross, adorned with carved work and with a high ascent of steps'.

Above left The base of Sturminster Newton's market cross. The area's wealth came from sheep and cattle, and the earliest grant of a fair in the town dates to 1219, during the reign of Henry III.

Left Stalbridge's medieval market cross is one of the finest in the country.

have been of the Priory and Castle rising above the surrounding rooftops.

No Dorset towns were important enough to require permanent defensive walls, but at Wareham and Dorchester the older Saxon and Roman walls respectively formed the town boundaries, while at Bridport boundary ditches around the Saxon and Norman towns provided a basic defensive line which could be further fortified if needed. Castles were built by the Normans at Dorchester, Shaftesbury, Corfe, Cranborne, Christchurch, and Sherborne as a show of dominance over their Saxon predecessors. Some never grew beyond motte and bailey structures, such as Christchurch, where the mound and ruins of the stone keep can still be viewed and enjoyed today. Sherborne's castle was outside the town and was more of a fortified palace than a structure intended for war. Only Corfe has left substantial remains beyond the end of the Middle Ages.

In all towns the focal point for both townspeople and incomers was the market square (which was often not square at all), at the meeting of the main roads into the town. The market square itself has frequently been reduced in size by encroachment and infill from later building. Within the square the location of trading sites was marked by a market cross. Some larger towns such as Shaftesbury had more than one cross, each marking where particular commodities were traded. In later centuries the cross itself was often removed, leaving just a base or stump.

At Sturminster Newton the road from the north opens out into a triangular market-place, now greatly reduced from its original size by later infilling. Close by is the base of the market cross. Sturminster developed from its minster origins to serve the neighbouring villages of the Blackmore Vale, but until the nineteenth century was largely a cluster of buildings around the market place.

Beaminster, another Saxon minster town, has a larger market place, possibly partly infilled on its northern side, with a memorial dating from 1906 standing on the site of its market cross; the town acquired its market charter in 1284.

Stalbridge shows how the position of market squares and crosses may not always have remained fixed during the Middle Ages. By 1200 much of the surrounding countryside was populated with farms and larger outlying settlements such as Stalbridge Weston and Stourton Caundle, each generating corn, wool, and dairy products, and creating the potential for a local market. In 1290 the Abbot of Sherborne, lord of the manor, had a grant of a Tuesday market and an annual fair, with a further fair granted in 1302. The original market place may have been at the crossroads at the foot of Barrow Hill, where there is a small triangular area which was later built over. The market cross now stands a little to the north along the main road, where the street widens, perhaps representing a later market site. The cross, of Ham Hill stone, has its arms missing, but is carved with depictions of the

Crucifixion and Resurrection, and is considered to be one of the finest surviving market crosses in the country.

Travellers arriving at Dorset's market towns would have noticed the regularly shaped burgage plots of the traders and principal townspeople. These were often laid out to a specific size, and characteristically extended backwards from the main street, forming blocks of strips, each with a narrow street frontage. Sometimes the size of burgage plots was laid down at the time of the town's foundation, as at Charmouth, where the plots were specified at the medieval equivalent of 110 by 20 metres. At Bridport the new Norman town was laid out north of the earlier Saxon settlement along the east-west main road now forming the High Street, formerly East and West Street. The burgage plots are shown on the map of 1799 as lying north and south from this road, those on the northern side extending as far as Rax Lane, which formed the northern boundary of the medieval town.

At Sherborne the 'new borough' of Newland lay east of the older town along the road between The Green and Castleton. An 1802 map shows surviving burgage strips extending back from this road. The burgages were long and thin, specified in the original charter as 120 or 100 by 20 metres. The map also marks a cross base at the end of a triangular strip of land, the site of the former market area, at that time infilled with later premises.

Visitors to Wimborne Minster might have noticed how the town seemed to lie in two distinct areas. Surrounding the huge minster church lay a cluster of irregular, narrow streets and alleyways. This area of the town had market sites in Cornmarket and High Street, and represents the original Saxon town which belonged to the dean of the minster. He received all the revenues from the markets held here and from the annual St. Cuthburga Fair. North of this area lay a quite different one, based on the two long parallel streets of West Borough and East Borough, and the planned creation of the lords of the manor of Kingston Lacy. Here there is evidence of former burgage plots extending backwards from West Borough, and visitors may have found a further market being held along this street, an alternative venue for buying and selling. This division of the town between dean and lord is still there for us to see today, just as it was to the visitor of a millennium ago.

Left West Borough, Wimborne, in about 1860. West Borough was laid out as a medieval extension to the Saxon town by the lords of the manor of Kingston Lacy as a way of raising money from tolls.

Right The Chantry, South St, Bridport, one of Dorset's few surviving medieval town houses.

Dorset towns have few buildings surviving from the Middle Ages. Houses were then largely of timber and thatch, and highly vulnerable to the ravages of fire. One surviving medieval house is The Chantry in Bridport, a fourteenth-century building which began life as the home of a priest and may also have been used to collect tolls from traders approaching the town. Another, of which only the ruins remain, is the Constable's House in Christchurch. This was built to house the

Christchurch from the air, 1975. Beyond the Priory are the ruins of the keep and the much-better preserved twelfth century Constable's House.

Pitchmarket, Abbey St, Cerne Abbas, a rare example of medieval timber-framed cottages 'jettied' out over the street.

constable or bailiff of the manor, and stood close to the castle. The remains suggest a substantial house with a solar over a ground floor storage area, roofed in stone and surrounded by timber buildings.

Surviving medieval houses in other English towns give us some idea of what those in Dorset were like. The better-off townsfolk had mostly detached houses, built at the street end of the burgage plot with the gable towards the street. The upper floor would be 'jettied', or overhanging the lower floor out over the street. The main room was a hall extending to the roof, with the shop premises fronting the street at one end and service rooms and private family rooms at the other. In Sherborne examples of medieval houses survive in Hound Street, Newland, and South Street, although much altered in later centuries. The latter example was a hall house of five bays or sections with stone walls and a collar-beam roof.

In many towns the rooflines of thatch and timber were dominated by the great structures of the abbeys and minster churches. At Abbotsbury and Cerne Abbas the abbey buildings dwarfed the towns which grew up alongside them. The tithe barn at Abbotsbury gives some indication of the wealth of the medieval abbey, while at Cerne Abbas in the fifteenth century the Guest Hall and a new barn were built, reflecting the abbey's continuing wealth. At Milton Abbas the

Two examples of the wealth of Dorset's monasteries are the Tithe Barn at Abbotsbury and the Guest House at Cerne Abbas.

great Saxon-Norman abbey was destroyed by fire in 1309, and although rebuilding started soon afterwards, it remained incomplete at the time of the Dissolution, and the townspeople became accustomed to seeing an abbey church without a nave and west end. The abbey towns also had parish churches for the use of the townspeople; that at Sherborne was attached to the western end of the abbey and its site can still be seen. Medieval records also mention other buildings linked to churches or charitable uses, such as chapels, hospices, leper

Hayter's Quay, Wareham, on the River Frome is the only reminder of the town's importance as a trading and shipbuilding port. The rise of Poole, the increased size and draught of boats combined with the gradual silting up of the Frome ended Wareham's days as a river port.

hospitals, and almshouses.

In a league table of medieval town importance, Shaftesbury emerges as the most populous town in Dorset, and its nunnery the wealthiest. The abbey was supported by extensive estates, and was rebuilt on a huge scale around 1100. As it grew in influence, so the medieval town at its gates prospered. The town spread eastwards from its Saxon 'burghal hidage' site towards the meeting point of north-south and east-west trade routes into the town. As a new network of streets developed, no fewer than twelve churches or chapels had come into existence by 1300 to serve the growing population.

A record known as the 'Dorchester Domesday' gives a glimpse into the economic life of a Dorset town in the fifteenth century by listing many of Dorchester's trades and occupations. There were butchers, bakers, skinners, tanners, glovers, saddlers, weavers, tailors, mercers, drapers, masons, carpenters, and smiths. Some trades were conspicuous by their absence but undoubtedly were there, such as brewers, dyers, and cornmongers. Many people owning and renting property in Dorchester came from outside the town, from Cerne Abbas, Weymouth, Sherborne, and even outside the county.

Apart from Weymouth Bay and Poole and Christchurch harbours, the Dorset coast has proved an obstacle to the development of maritime trade. The high steep cliffs and many small coves provide few safe anchorages. The early ports of Bridport, Christchurch, and Wareham, although having access to the sea, were river ports rather than coastal ones. Bridport, a mile and a half upstream, had no reliable harbour for many centuries. Wareham remained Dorset's main port until the early fourteenth century, after which it underwent a rapid decline. It last supplied ships for the king in 1347, but thereafter ceases to be mentioned as a port. The decline may be due to the silting of the river, the rise of Poole, and perhaps also the Black Death, which was clearly virulent in Wareham since it killed seven priests in 1348.

The earliest drawing of Lyme Regis, from 'The Bird's Eye View of the Dorset Coast', 1539. 'The Cobbe of Lyme' was originally built of wooden piles and blocks of stone to provide shelter from the prevailing south-westerly wind. The town sits huddled beneath the beacon on Black Ven.

Weymouth Harbour. The two towns of Melcombe Regis and Weymouth developed either side of the mouth of the River Wey. Confusingly, what we think of as Weymouth today, with its Esplanade and beach, was originally Melcombe Regis.

By this time the growth in maritime trade was passing to a new generation of coastal towns. Lyme Regis, in Saxon times a small village based on saltworking, grew into a port of consequence despite having no natural harbour. Its success was due to the construction of the Cobb, a breakwater which produced an artificial bay where ships could be safely loaded. In 1284 Edward I made Lyme a free borough, by which time it was heavily involved in the French wine trade. Like other ports, Lyme supplied ships for the navy, and in 1293 the town was required to build a boat of 120 oars. In 1331 it was 'inhabited by . . . rich and powerful merchants owning fifteen great ships and forty boats.' But Lyme's success was short-lived: by 1378 it was 'for the most part destroyed and wasted by the sea . . . the Cobb having been swept away . . .' Storms, French wars, and possibly onsets of plague ensured little revival until Tudor times.

Located on opposite sides of the mouth of the River Wey, but in different parishes and lordships, Melcombe Regis and Weymouth both originated as new planned towns in the mid-thirteenth century. The natural anchorages of Weymouth Bay and Radipole Lake, together with the protection offered by Chesil Beach, made it an ideal site for a harbour. Weymouth, on the south side, had the more constricted site, on a narrow strip of land contained by cliffs. Melcombe Regis, by contrast, occupied a wide, level alluvial peninsula which allowed the laying out of a grid-iron street plan, which still survives. Both towns prospered from the wool trade, with Melcombe

The Town Cellars (Wool House) and Customs House, Poole Quay. The Town Cellars were once much larger and used for storing wool, but remain one of the best examples of a medieval woolhouse in Britain. The elegant Custom House with its matching flights of curved steps was built in 1813.

Regis becoming the Port of the Staple. But it was also the port of entry for the Black Death in 1348, and must have suffered greatly as a result. Both towns were devastated by French raids, and in 1400 Melcombe Regis asked for its rent to the king to be reduced, claiming that the wealthy merchants had now all left. In 1433 the port was closed, 'for lack and scarcity of help of people to withstand the king's enemies'.

The early decline of Wareham owed much to the rise of Poole, located closer to the entrance to Poole Harbour and better placed for coastal and continental trade. Later development makes it difficult to appreciate the almost island site of medieval Poole, occupying the end of a peninsula jutting out into Poole Harbour, separated from the mainland by a boggy, tidal creek. Unlike Melcombe Regis, there is no evidence of regular planning, and the early town clustered around the old market place by the Quay. The areas around Thames Street and Strand Street date from this time, with long, narrow alleys between Strand Street and the Quay marking the boundaries between medieval warehouses. The Town Cellars (Wool House) and Scaplens Court are the only surviving buildings from this time.

By the fifteenth century Poole had become the largest port between Southampton and Exeter, with its prosperity based on exports of wool and imports of continental wine and other commodities. As with other Dorset ports, the fifteenth century brought troubles and decline, including being sacked by a French and Spanish raid, and a decline in the wool trade. It was the sixteenth century before Dorset's seaports could find a renewed prosperity.

TAXATION AND PROSPERITY

Taxation records give us some indication of the relative prosperity and size of Dorset's medieval towns. In 1332, when a lay subsidy was levied across the county, Sherborne, Shaftesbury, and Milton Abbas headed the list of taxpayers. Shaftesbury was easily the wealthiest, and was almost as wealthy as Weymouth and Bridport, the next two contenders, combined. Dorchester ranked seventh in population size, while the 'new' boroughs created in the thirteenth century were all much smaller. Weymouth, Melcombe Regis, Poole, and Wareham, being ports, were more heavily taxed than the inland towns.

The taxation records only tell part of the story, for many townsfolk were too poor to pay tax. Dorchester was bigger than it might appear, for it was largely surrounded by the populous manor of Fordington, which although taxed separately, was almost a suburb. Within each town there could be great variations in levels of wealth; half of the tax raised in Wareham in 1332 was contributed by only four individuals.

Looked at on the wider scale, Dorset's towns were all relatively small. Shaftesbury came only fifth in a 'wealth table' of towns in south-west England in 1334. The list was headed by Salisbury, which almost quadrupled Shaftesbury in wealth. Other Dorset towns were even poorer, the richest merchants of Weymouth, Wareham, and Poole in 1332 trailing well behind their rivals in Southampton and Bristol.

FROM TUDOR TO REGENCY

From Tudor times to the early nineteenth century some towns grew in size and importance while others declined. By the early sixteenth century Dorchester had become the most populous town in the county, followed by Shaftesbury, Sherborne, Milton Abbas, and Bridport. But by the time of the first census in 1801 they had all edged further down the rankings list, which was now headed by Poole and Weymouth. Cerne Abbas, ranked sixth around 1500, had fallen to almost the bottom of the list and had almost ceased to be a town at all.

The fortunes of some towns were affected by the Reformation. The Dissolution of the religious houses promptly ended the steady influx of pilgrims and visitors and the money they brought with them. The monastic houses had also provided work through the many trades and businesses needed to keep them in good repair and supply their daily needs. At Christchurch, the immediate impact of the Dissolution is clearly visible in an unfinished section of parapet construction on the top of one of the walls. The poorer townspeople suffered the further

Dorchester from the east in 1770. Fordington is on the left, as is Grey's Bridge over the River Frome, which was built in 1748 to take the new London road across the water meadows.

loss of almsgiving and charitable works, until that time an important social role of the monasteries. In some towns the setback seems to have been only temporary, and by the mid-sixteenth century they were thriving once more. Some, like Sherborne, gained the abbey church for the use of the townspeople. At Abbotsbury and Cerne Abbas the blow was far heavier, with both towns going into decline.

Plague also took its toll. At Wimborne Minster the increased number of burials in 1625 points to an outbreak. It returned again in 1638, causing up to 400 dead, many of whom were buried in common graves in St. Peter's churchyard, now under the town Square. Workmen still find occasional bones when digging here. This latter outbreak decimated the cloth trade, which never recovered.

One Dorset town ceased to exist altogether. Milton Abbas, having weathered the Reformation and the loss of its monastery, eventually fell victim two centuries later to Joseph Damer, Viscount Milton and later Earl of Dorchester. Having rebuilt his house at Milton Abbey in a grand classical style, he then demolished most of the town in order to make way for a landscaped park. The population was rehoused in a new model village, now one of the best-known villages in Dorset. The site of the old town is still to be found, with the main streets and the sites of several houses still visible.

Some travellers through Dorset give glimpses of the ups and downs in urban prosperity. In 1542 John Leland noted the importance of the fishing trade in Lyme Regis, the presence of merchants from Brittany, and the shelter provided by the Cobb. At Bridport he commented on the lack of a proper harbour. Of Melcombe Regis he wrote, 'there are evident signs that this town was formerly much larger than it is now, and this is attributed to the French, who during times of war took advantage of its lack of defences and razed it.' By contrast, the defences at Weymouth, just across the water, were in better shape: 'barely a mile along the shore from the harbour mouth has been built an excellent castle equipped for war, with one open barbican.'

Another traveller, Celia Fiennes, visited Dorset during the last decades of the seventeenth century. Blandford Forum she described as a 'pretty neat country town', while Poole was a 'little sea-port town' with 'a very good minister in the public church.'

A few years later, Daniel Defoe's route from London to Land's End

High West Street, Dorchester, from Top o'Town, in an engraving that captures the genteel provincial character of Dorset's county town in the early nineteenth century. The mounted soldier was probably returning to the Marabout Barracks, built in 1795 for the Dorset Yeomanry.

took him through several Dorset towns, including Dorchester. Speed's map of a century earlier shows it clearly contained within its old Roman walls, and by Defoe's time it was still much the same size. However, as the county town, it was beginning to acquire a more defined social standing. Defoe found it to be 'a pleasant, agreeable town to live in', and although Dorchester society was divided in its religion and politics, it was nevertheless a place where ministers of different denominations might be expected to converse 'with good civility and neighbourhood.' He noted that 'there is good company, and a great deal of it' and that 'time could be agreeably spent in Dorchester as in any other town in England'. High West Street developed as the fashionable part of the town centre, and later in the century the Roman walls around the south and west sides of the town made way for the tree-lined walks which are still so attractive today.

TRADE, COMMERCE, AND TRAVEL

At this time some twenty towns in Dorset had regular markets. Throughout the south of England markets revived after the upheavals of the Civil War, many towns recording peaks in their market tolls in

The Fish Cross and stocks, Shaftesbury.

the 1690s, and numbers remained fairly constant until the end of the eighteenth century.

The markets held in the smaller towns and villages were of little more than local significance, but others, like Shaftesbury, had a wider importance. On its market day some fifty shambles or market stalls were spread around the main streets. Court cases and trading records mention huge quantities of corn and large numbers of cattle, sheep, swine, and poultry. The crosses marking the trading sites are shown on a plan of the town from 1615. A Butter Cross stood in the area later known as the Commons, and a Fish Cross at the top of Gold Hill. Corn and cereals were traded in the area of the Cornmarket, the present-day High Street, and along Oatmell Row. Sheep were sold on Gold Hill and on Bleke Street; cattle, driven from Wales, were traded on Bimport after being grazed in the Park on the old Abbey grounds. A new Guildhall was built in 1569 on The Commons at a site just in front of the present Town Hall.

Shaftesbury had the advantage of being located where the east-west road from London to the West Country crossed the north-south route between Bristol and Poole. Its prominent hill-top position made it a natural focus for people on the move, and in the early seventeenth century the population was swollen by migrants and vagrants from the countryside seeking relief from poverty. Wheeled traffic increased, leading to disputes over obstruction between stallholders and travellers, eventually bringing about the demolition of Oatmell Row and removal

Blandford Forum market in 1790, by Thomas Rowlandson. On the left is the London coach, which took 12 hours to reach the city. The Saturday market was known for lace, buttons and a 'great stock of butcher's meat'.

of the Butter Cross to give more room for loaded vehicles. Outside the old medieval town, at the foot of the steep slope which had once marked the town's Anglo-Saxon defences, the St. James area flourished as a neighbourhood of small trades and businesses. This busy, bustling town was noted for its large number of inns, of which there were 27 during the eighteenth century. The town itself was gradually rebuilt incorporating stone from the former abbey, now a convenient quarry used by builders and townsfolk alike.

Markets like Shaftesbury flourished on the produce of the surrounding countryside, the town being mid-way between the rolling chalklands of eastern and central Dorset and the rich claylands of the Blackmore Vale. Throughout Dorset the many chalkland villages were producers of corn and wool, the manure from the large flocks of sheep kept on the downs being used to fertilise the cornfields. By contrast in the north and west of the county, particularly in the clay lands of the Vales of Blackmore and Marshwood, farming was based on the production of milk turned into butter and cheese, and the rearing of cattle and pigs. Cattle were also brought into the region to be fattened, mainly from Wales and Ireland. In the heathland regions bordering the

The old Weymouth Town Hall and market shambles in John Nixon's watercolour of 1790 were later demolished to make way for the Guildhall.

New Forest and around Poole Harbour, cattle and horse rearing were especially important. This diversity of produce found its way on to the stalls and streets of the market towns, producing distinctive varieties such as the 'Blue Vinny' cheeses of the Blackmore Vale.

The market stalls were laden not just with local farm produce but also with the output of trades and crafts. In the livestock rearing areas of the county, people had long turned to secondary occupations to add to their income, and their local towns also became involved in these industries. Silk weaving flourished around Sherborne in the seventeenth century, providing employment both in mills and for outworkers. Lace was made at Lyme Regis and Blandford, with Defoe claiming in around 1720 that Blandford Forum was 'chiefly famous for making the finest bonelace in England.' Other textile and clothing-related industries such as bonnet making, stocking knitting, glove making, and button making were also widespread. These trades provided livelihoods for women and girls, often in their own homes, but nothing now remains of their former importance.

Sturminster Newton was notable for its manufacture of swanskin, a tough, coarse cloth favoured by the Newfoundland fishermen, many of whom were recruited from Sturminster. The manufacture may have been introduced by groups of Huguenot refugees in the sixteenth century, and used a fulling mill which shared the site of the better-known corn mill. The industry reached its height of production in the 1790s when it employed nearly three hundred people, but appears to have died out early in the next century.

In west Dorset linen, sailcloth, ropes, and nets were produced in and around Beaminster, Broadwindsor, and Bridport. The industry had its origins in the growth of flax and hemp in the rich, damp soils of the area. Hutchins' *History of Dorset* chronicles the significance of the rope and nets industry of Bridport: 'Since the year 1720 a great many brick houses have been built here, and the streets well paved . . . upwards of 1500 tons of hemp and flax are worked up annually.' These industries flourished by meeting the demands of the Newfoundland fishing fleets operating out of Dorset, and also by supplying the Royal Navy. At Bridport the impact of the rope industry is especially well marked in the many rope-walks found around the town, long strips of land where the threads could be stretched out before being spun into a rope. In South Street, doorways between the houses give access on to long, narrow gardens or alleyways, sometimes now partly covered with sheds, but formerly used as rope-walks.

Wimborne Minster shows something of the variety of occupations

Bridport in the 1830s. The town's boom years lay ahead. As well as supplying sailcloth, sacking, nets and twine to the Royal Navy, merchant shipping and fishing fleet, the town's products were soon being exported all over the world to the new colonies of the emerging British Empire.

The old Market House in the Cornmarket, Wimborne Minster.

and livelihoods in a Dorset town in the seventeenth century. The main craft, although becoming less important as the century progressed, was the textile trade, employing clothiers, tailors, weavers, and fullers. There were particular specialist textile crafts such as flax dressers, wool combers, collar workers, or ropers. Many of these trades, together with leather working, were to be found in the Borough area. Around the town there were dealers in wool, livestock, corn, and building materials. Most retail trades operated from within the permitted market areas in Market Street (High Street) and around the Cornmarket. In 1758 the new Market House was built on the site of the old Guildhall. Wimborne was also notable for its attorneys, lawyers, and notaries, possibly reflecting the work generated by the courts of the church, manor, and hundred, and nearness to the Quarter Sessions at Poole.

Despite the poor state of many of the roads of the time, regular carrier and packhorse services linked towns, countryside, and the wider region beyond. Fish was regularly carried by pack-horses from Poole and Lyme Regis to London, Oxford, Devizes, and elsewhere. Carriers returning from London brought luxury goods, silk, and haberdasheries, items appealing to the wealthier townspeople and local gentry eager to follow the latest fashions and designs from the capital.

From the mid-eighteenth century turnpike roads made carrier services more regular and reliable, and particularly speeded up the coaches and mails, giving towns faster links with each other. The system was best developed around Poole and Wareham, and also around Dorchester and Sherborne, but much of central and western Dorset remained outside the network. A route of importance was the turnpike road from Salisbury to Blandford, Dorchester, and Bridport, which greatly reduced the time needed to cross Cranborne Chase. Some towns found a new importance as coaching stops, reflected in the imposing coaching inns which are still part of their high streets. In 1840, on the eve of the railway age, the Crown Hotel at Blandford could boast regular direct services, some daily, to London, Portsmouth, Brighton, Southampton, Bath, Bristol, Exeter, Plymouth, Falmouth, Weymouth, and Poole.

By contrast the small town of Cranborne, which had been an important stopping point on the older road system, lost out to the turnpike era. The town had already been in decline for a century since the manor courts of Cranborne Chase had been moved to Wimborne St. Giles. Although it gained a turnpike link from Wimborne Minster, it was entirely by-passed once the new Great Western turnpike from Salisbury to Blandford road was built, and found its coaching traffic fade away. In 1815 the market was described as 'nearly lost' and the market house itself was pulled down in 1828.

THE COASTAL TOWNS

Thomas Gerard's *Survey of Dorsetshire* of 1622 (but not published until 1723 under the name of John Coker) tells us that 'on the south shore . . . (are the) three good haven towns of Lyme, Weymouth, and Poole.' In the seventeenth century all three towns had been linked as a 'Port of Poole' with its customs headquarters at Poole. All of them experienced varying fortunes.

Poole, a great wool exporting port in late medieval times, saw its exports slump in the sixteenth century before finding a new prosperity from the growing Newfoundland fishing trade. In this 'triangle of trade' ships from Poole carried salt to Newfoundland, salted cod was then shipped to the Mediterranean, the ships returning to Poole with Mediterranean products such as wine and olive oil. By 1802 there were 350 ships in the Poole fleet. A walk around the old streets of Poole provides ample evidence of the wealth brought into the town. Here can be found the many Georgian mansions and public buildings built by the leading merchants, with good examples around Thames Street and Church Street. The Poole merchants founded whole dynasties and through intermarriage formed an elite group of 'merchant princes.' Poole's best known building is the Custom House, built in 1813 to replace one built in 1747 and destroyed by fire. Another building symbolic of Poole's wealth is the Guildhall of 1761, with its market shops below and corporation chamber and courtroom above. Yet even with this prosperity the town was still confined to the small peninsula on which it had first grown up.

Lyme Regis, although smaller than Poole, continued to flourish throughout the seventeenth century. Its coastal trade developed and new routes were opened up to Africa and America. An account of 1635 referred to the 'rare and unparalleled harbour called the Cobb, wherein . . . (could be found) 30 and 40 good vessels, and of a pretty burthen . . . all safely lodged and bosomed'. But the same writer also noticed the 'stony and craggy way into Lyme', which meant that most access into the town was on horseback. The steepness of slopes for wheeled vehicles, together with the confined space for expansion, were to prove limitations to any further growth as a port in the longer run. The cost of maintaining the Cobb became a drain on the town's resources and the harbour became too small for larger shipping, although some shipbuilding continued. The decline continued, so that by 1750, to quote George Roberts, Lyme's first historian, 'The population had dwindled to one thousand inhabitants, so that a great number of buildings remained unoccupied, and were so neglected that it is an incontestible fact that no one could walk with safety in the streets during a high wind, which frequently blew down the most tottering buildings. The only ways out of the town were by narrow lanes, full of deep ruts; the streets, almost impassable for carriages, were the abode chiefly of very poor people, who earned a scanty subsistence by their several trades.'

By the early nineteenth century Lyme's fortunes had reversed, and

Stone urns and pineapples decorate the baroque façade of West End House, Poole, built by the Newfoundland merchant John Slade in about 1740.

The Guildhall, Poole, as depicted on the painted inn sign of the nearby Guildhall Arms.

Marine Parade, Lyme Regis, an engraving of 1833 showing the promenade laid out by the philanthropist Thomas Hollis in the 1770s.

it had taken on a completely new character as a watering place for fashionable Bath society, well known to readers of Jane Austen as a 'pleasant little bay, which in the season is animated with bathing machines and company.' From this period date the many attractive town houses with their classical style frontages, elegant porches, and cast-iron balconies, which jostle next to each other along the Marine Parade and still define the character of the town.

In 1571 Weymouth and Melcombe Regis became united into one town, after centuries of quarrelling over harbour dues, ownership of the water between them, and the right to erect quays. Even after amalgamation the quarrels continued and during the Civil War the two sides found themselves on opposite sides, exchanging cannon fire and fireships in 1645. Although the name 'Weymouth' subsequently triumphed for the whole town, it was nevertheless Melcombe which became the commercial centre, and today it is the old streets of Melcombe around St. Thomas Street and St. Mary Street where the town's major shops are to be found.

The history of Weymouth and Melcombe entered a new phase in 1773 when a Bath developer, Andrew Sproule, opened a hotel and new Assembly Rooms outside the old town of Melcombe on the edge of the beach on a site occupied by the later Royal Hotel. In 1780 the Duke of Gloucester, George III's younger brother, built himself the

Top Gloucester Lodge, the holiday home on Weymouth Esplanade of George III and his family. The shell of the building still survives as part of the Gloucester Hotel.

Above Weymouth Esplanade. In the centre, behind the statue of George III, are Royal Terrace and Frederick Place, both of which stand on the site of the former gardens of Gloucester Lodge.

seafront residence still known as Gloucester Lodge. From 1789 George III stayed regularly at Gloucester Lodge, and continued to visit every year until 1805, securing the town's status as a fashionable resort, and the practice of sea-bathing as an acceptable social habit. The King's daily bathing ritual, involving his elaborate bathing machine and a band of musicians, became the focus of attention in the town during his visits. The statue of the king at the entrance to the old town, erected by 'The grateful inhabitants to George III', leaves no doubt of the importance of the royal connection.

The town quickly spread beyond its medieval confines, with the building of the Esplanade along the shore. A walk along it today takes in the fine rows and terraces between Royal Crescent and Devonshire Buildings, all from around 1800. 'Roundhouses' were later built to give style to the ends of Johnstone Row and Coburg Place. The rest of the seafront grew piece by piece later in the century: Royal Terrace 1816-18, Brunswick Terrace 1827, Waterloo Place 1835, and Victoria Terrace 1850.

FIRES AND REBUILDING

By the eighteenth century Dorset's towns were undergoing a transformation. The 'old and low' buildings noticed by Defoe in Dorchester, and widespread elsewhere, were giving way to taller, more substantial properties built in stone or brick and often displaying the latest tastes in architectural style. The rebuilding was furthered by a growing urban prosperity, especially among the gentry, merchant, and professional classes, who had the wealth to invest in new or rebuilt homes providing more space and comforts.

Rebuilding was also hastened by fire, then a periodic, almost inevitable hazard. Gillingham has so few older buildings because of a fire in 1694. In Sturminster Newton some buildings around the market place bear the datestone 1730, reflecting new building following a disastrous fire in 1729.

Beaminster had fires in 1644, 1684, 1781, and 1786. The 1644 fire was started by the discharge of a musket into the roof of a house during the Civil War. One observer wrote on the blank leaf of his Bible that 'it was wild fire and the wind being directly with the town, so that the whole town was all destroyed in two hours . . . there were seven score and four dwelling houses besides barns and stables burnt'. Only East Street and part of Church Street escaped.

When the future Charles II hurried through Beaminster in 1654 on his flight from Charmouth he was 'so struck by the melancholy aspect of the place that he would not halt there as he intended . . .' Thirty years later fire returned to level much of the town yet again, including the Town Hall. A plaque on another Beaminster house records: 'This Towne burnt in 1684 . . . Howse rebuilt in 1687. W.L.'

Left Eastway House, Blandford, a Georgian town house built in 1735.

Right The old Greyhound Inn, Blandford, rebuilt by the Bastard brothers after the 1731 fire. The superb stucco façade is generally regarded as the best surviving example of urban English Baroque architecture.

Perhaps the best known of Dorset fires is the great fire of Blandford Forum in 1731. The intensity of the fire can be felt in the graphic account of the Reverend Malachi Blake, who took obvious Puritan relish at the evidence of God's rebuking hand, and concluded that 'Man is born into trouble as the sparks fly upwards.' The fire is historically significant for what happened afterwards. The aftermath provided a survey map showing the detailed layout of the town at the time of the fire; a property valuation revealing the huge gap in wealth between the rich and the poor; and the eventual outcome of the rebuilding itself. This rebuilding provided one of the finest examples in England of an eighteenth-century market town.

The reconstruction of Blandford was largely supervised by the architect brothers John and William Bastard, who personally designed the larger, more important buildings and oversaw the work of lesser builders around the town. The result is a mix of uniformity and diversity, with a common use of brick types and bondings, a blending and zoning of buildings based on social class, and the skilful use of

The interior of Bridport's Unitarian chapel of 1794.

classical techniques such as street vistas, symmetrical elevations, and a range of ornamental features. Although the ground level around the market place has now been taken over by modern shop frontages, the achievements of the Bastards can be enjoyed by looking above the street level and wandering into the streets and alleyways behind the church.

Rebuilding normally followed wealth and social status. At the top end of the social ladder this meant the better-off middle and professional classes such as lawyers, doctors, architects, property owners, prosperous tradesmen, and those of private means. They were able to buy high quality stone and brick and to employ architects and builders with pattern books containing the latest architectural styles. Their influence is best seen in some of the larger houses of Blandford, Poole, and Weymouth.

Eastway House, East Street, Blandford, built in 1735, is a typical high quality Georgian town house with a carefully proportioned symmetrical frontage, sash windows, urns on the roof, elaborate pilasters and decorative fanlight over the door. At Weymouth the same layer of society was responsible for the many Georgian terraces of the Esplanade area such as the Royal Crescent, an imposing sweep of 15 houses originally intended as a larger run of 49 properties.

Further down the social scale rebuilding often occurred in a less ostentatious way. At Wareham, largely rebuilt in the late eighteenth century after a fire, prominent houses with fine Georgian features mingle with more modest cottages, sometimes displaying a mix of rendered brickwork, symmetrical double frontage, tiled roofs, and sash windows. At Lyme Regis Georgian features are common on the houses along the Marine Parade, but in the streets leading uphill out of the town the buildings are in a simpler, more vernacular style with plain frontages and doorways, and the occasional oriel window or cast iron balcony. In Cerne Abbas, in the streets around the old abbey site, rebuilding took place over a period of time; several houses have Georgian frontages but older structures behind, some still retaining the jettying of Tudor times.

CHURCHES, CHARITIES, AND SCHOOLS

Parish churches continued to play a central role in social and religious life. This was not a time when many new churches were built, although there are notable exceptions such as the new Georgian church in Blandford Forum following the fire. It was rather a period when population growth stretched the capacity of some churches to their limits, and when the interiors of churches and the conduct of services was affected by changes in doctrine and liturgy. Box pews and galleries became widespread. The church at Castleton, near Sherborne, built in 1714, was planned as a 'preaching' church with a small recess for a chancel and a gallery for musicians.

By the eighteenth century the established church was being challenged by Dissent. At Wareham and Bridport in 1770 over half the families were Presbyterian, Nonconformist, or other non-Anglican denominations. In Dorchester there were Dissenter meeting houses in Colliton Street and Durngate Street. In Bridport the Unitarian chapel of 1794 still has its original side galleries, pews, and central pulpit; also in Bridport in South Street is the Quaker Meeting House of 1697, still in use. Dissent was not always readily tolerated; at Wimborne Minster the weavers of shalloons (a closely woven type of cloth), all Dissenters, were dismissed for not attending church, and so were

Left Napper's Mite Almshouses, Dorchester, established in 1615 to house 10 'poor men'.

Right William Lush's Blue Coat School, Bell Street, Shaftesbury, was originally founded by a mercer to teach 20 poor boys and girls. Once educated, Lush's will also paid for the children to be apprenticed to local tradesmen or to the Newfoundland fishery based in Poole.

forced to move to Romsey, where conditions were more tolerant.

After the Reformation private charities replaced the abbeys as the main providers of education and social care. In Dorchester three charities were founded following the fire of 1613; 'when they saw by this sudden blast great buildings turned into heaps of stones ... many men's bowels began to yearn in compassion.' Wimborne Minster benefited from numerous charities in the sixteenth and seventeenth centuries, such as Collett's charity of 1621 for ten poor persons of 'good and honest fame'. In Dorchester the Napper's Mite Almshouses in South Street were established in 1615 out of the will of Sir Robert Napier, also for ten poor men. The establishment of the charity followed soon after the great Dorchester fire of 1613, seen by some as a scourge sent by God to punish the uncharitable population. Another almshouse linked with fire is the Ryves Almshouse in Blandford Forum, founded in 1682. This was one of the few buildings to survive the fire of 1731, no doubt seen by many as a vindication of the good works carried out under its roof.

Schools also started to appear in some towns, but only a small number of children had access to any form of education, much of which was rudimentary. In Gillingham in 1516 a trust was formed 'that out of the issues and profits thereof, there might be perpetually maintained . . . a Schoolmaster, for instruction of the youth in good literature, for the better discharge of their duty to God, the King and the Commonwealth.' Such was the beginnings of the Gillingham Free School, later the Grammar School. In nearby Shaftesbury William Lush's school was founded soon after 1700 on a site now occupied by 47 Bell Street. It intended to provide a start in life for twenty poor boys and girls, but in the event only boys were taken in. The charity paid for the indenturing of its pupils, when their education was finished, to local tradesmen or to the Newfoundland fisheries; and also the clothing of boys not only while at school but also during their apprenticeship. In Blandford the Blue-Coat School was founded from a charity of William Wake, an Archbishop of Canterbury born in Blandford, to provide a schoolmaster to teach twelve poor boys to a curriculum which included accounts and navigation, possibly expecting them to be taken on by Poole merchants involved in the Newfoundland trade.

One town in which schools made a particularly lasting impact was Sherborne, so much so that schools almost became a 'main industry' of the town, helping to define its personality. There had been a medieval grammar school under the patronage of the monastery, and this was refounded by Edward VI in 1550; at this time new schools were looked on favourably by the monarchy as a way of fostering the new Protestantism. The original site within the abbey precinct was later added to by new buildings. In another endowment in 1640, Richard Foster left land for 'the better education and breeding up of ten poor boys and ten poor maids . . . to be instructed to read the English tongue'. The school eventually became known as the 'blue school' from the colour of the boys' coats, which were similar to those worn in London charity schools, and no 'maids' appeared until 1738.

Queen Elizabeth Grammar School, Wimborne. The school was established in 1563, rebuilt in mock-Elizabethan style in 1850 and has now been converted into flats.

Yet a further school was founded in 1743 from Lord Digby's endowment to the Brethren of the Almshouse for a school for thirteen poor girls.

By Regency times, Dorset's towns were larger, more substantial, and more prosperous than they had been at the time of the Reformation. The wealth and well-being of their inhabitants depended on the prosperity of the surrounding countryside, their trades and crafts, and their markets. A new middle class had appeared, wealthy enough to build itself more comfortable homes and with the time to spend exchanging views on religion and politics in the assembly rooms of fashionable towns like Weymouth. The contrast between the wealthy few and the rest of the townspeople was nowhere more true than in the churches. Here the appearance of box pews reflected the deep divisions in society, 'so that the wealthy sit at their ease, or kneel upon cushions, while the poor stand during the whole services.'

VICTORIAN EXPANSION

Between 1831 and 1901 the population of Dorset increased from 159,000 to 200,000, but the growth was uneven. A few towns developed at a tremendous rate, while the smaller towns and rural communities scarcely expanded at all, or after initial growth declined sharply later in the century. Leading the growth was Bournemouth, at that time in Hampshire and a place unknown to most people in southern England until after 1850, but then mushrooming from a few hundred people to well over 60,000 in 1901. Portland, acquiring a growing sprawl of quarrying villages, trebled its population during the final half of the century, with parts of it becoming more like a town. The old market towns of the chalklands all lost population after 1850, Beaminster seeing its population drop from 2,832 in 1851 to 1,702 in 1901. The even more rural Cerne Abbas saw its 1851 population of 1,343 more than halved over the same period.

Widespread migration from Dorset's countryside towards its bigger towns lay behind much of the changing pattern of population. Growing rural poverty led many families to leave Dorset altogether for the expanding towns of the industrial north or Midlands, or even the beckoning new world across the Atlantic. But there was also a steady drift of people to the south coast ports, seaside resorts, and to towns with military establishments. Here there was the likelihood of work in quarrying, the building industries, or harbour and railway construction. The booming holiday trade which arrived with the railways brought further jobs in catering and services. In some towns the coming of steam power gave older industries a new lease of life. The steam age increased productiveness in breweries and tanneries, ushered in a period of factory production amongst the rope and nets industries of Bridport, and speeded up the exporting of Purbeck stone from Portland and Swanage. These developments provided some hope of livelihoods for people driven out of the rural districts by growing

West Bay was one of the last places in Dorset to be linked to the railway network (1884), and it was also amongst the first to close (passengers 1930, goods 1960).

agricultural depression and poverty.

The arrival of the railway also affected the prosperity of towns. The railway first reached Wimborne and Dorchester in 1847 in the 'Railway Mania' years, but other towns had to wait for a rail link. By 1862 nearly every important market town – with the notable exceptions of Shaftesbury and Lyme Regis – had its railway. Because of the hilly terrain, it took until 1903 before Lyme was finally linked to the system. Towns on the railway network became the 'winners' of the railway age, able to think in terms of wider, even national, markets for their products. In the north of the county the dairy towns of the Blackmore Vale began sending milk to the London market; in the south the railway opened up the coast to holidaymakers and day-trippers, transforming Weymouth, Bournemouth, and Swanage into booming resorts within a few years of its arrival.

The trade directories of the period are a way of learning more about the growing commercial diversity of Dorset's towns. In 1823 Melcombe Regis, which still considered itself to be separate from Weymouth, could boast some 240 tradesmen or business people in 60 different trades or professions; by 1844 the numbers had risen to 400 and 85 respectively, and this was before the holiday business took off later in the century.

The rural market towns were largely self-sufficient, also servicing the needs of the neighbouring agricultural population. The Post Office Directory for Beaminster in 1875 listed 169 commercial entries, with some traders having more than one business. One especially diverse entry was that of Edwin Coombs, 'draper, millwright, timber merchant, stamp distributor, and clerk to the commissioners of the Bridport turnpike trust.' Some family businesses established in the Victorian period, or before, survived through into modern times; notable examples in Beaminster were the Pine grocery business, which traded there from 1787 to 1987, and the Hine pharmacy, which dispensed medicines to the townsfolk for 135 years. In towns without a railway link the carrier played an important role in providing transport to the nearest station; in Beaminster Alfred Woodbury was 'Agent for goods and parcels of the Great Western Railway Company' and his wagon left daily for Bridport at 9 am.

Inns and alehouses were much more numerous than they are today. Hostelries varied from the superior coaching inns, already long established, to the backstreet beer houses, many of which came into existence only after 1830. In Bridport several houses in South Street were used as beerhouses, some being no more than a room in an ordinary house. Some Bridport innkeepers were also involved in the rope trade, for example the Hope and Anchor in St. Michael's Lane, where twine spinning was carried on in rooms behind the bar. The arrival of the railway meant that beer could now be bought profitably from breweries outside the town.

A new generation of church and public building led the changing appearance of towns. After 1840 many medieval churches were rebuilt or replaced by larger, imposing Gothic-styled buildings better equipped to accommodate growing congregations. In Gillingham the Reverend Henry Deane, a dedicated builder of new churches in north Dorset, contributed £550 of his own money to taking down all but the medieval chancel and replacing it with a larger, high nave with galleries, providing space in the church for more than 1,100 people. In Shaftesbury Holy Trinity church was rebuilt in 1841 with an embattled tower 100 feet high, still the most striking feature on the Shaftesbury skyline.

Nonconformists shared in the rush to rebuild churches. By 1850 one in fifteen of the population attended Methodist services at 147 places of worship throughout the county. Gillingham Wesleyans and Primitive Methodists both opened new Gothic-style chapels in the 1870s. In Bridport the new Methodist chapel of 1860, already built with school rooms, soon proved to be too small and needed five extra rooms within a few years. In Christchurch the Dissenters' Meeting House, a seventeenth century building which had been built out of a barn, was itself replaced in 1867 by the Congregational Church, to which were added a lecture hall and schoolroom.

Once the railways began to reduce the cost of transporting building materials, timber and thatch began to disappear in favour of brick, stone, and slate, and the Victorian working-class terrace made its appearance. Certain towns bear the imprint of particular individuals. A notable example was Richard Grosvenor, Marquis of Westminster, and owner of most of Shaftesbury. He provided the town with a new water supply, market hall, corn and produce market, and cattle market. He repaired and rebuilt much of the High Street and adjoining streets, using a mix of red brick and local greensand stone – materials which still dominate the town.

Some towns retained an air of genteel decadence, not willing to notice the wider changes of the period. Wimborne Minster was notable for 'the gentlemen, shopkeepers, and better sorts of individuals in and about the town.' James Druitt, one of a Wimborne-Christchurch family of lawyers and surgeons who had practised in Wimborne for generations, described in his writings the 'small society' of the town in the 1830s, whose members used to pass the winter evenings entertaining each other dancing the quadrille or playing whist.

HARDY'S DORCHESTER

Thomas Hardy knew Dorchester intimately and made use of it widely in many of his novels and stories. As a young man he would walk each day from his home in neighbouring Bockhampton across the meadows by the River Frome and up East Street to his work as an apprentice architect with John Hicks in his office in South Street. One of the buildings he helped Hicks restore was the medieval church of St Peter,

All that survives of Dorchester's Poor Law Union Workhouse of 1837 is the east entrance wing, now part of the Dorset County Hospital.

which stands prominently in the High Street. He also met the poet William Barnes, who ran a school next door to Hicks' office. At this time Dorchester was still very much within its Georgian limits, its extent defined by the old Roman walls converted into tree-lined walks a century earlier. Today the walks still give a feel of the leisurely character of the town and the slower pace of life of Hardy's time.

Dorchester also had its less salubrious parts. In *The Mayor of Casterbridge* Hardy refers to an area he calls 'Durnover' with a street named 'Mixen Lane', places which he links with squalor and low life. The real locations were Fordington and Mill Street, and the unwholesome conditions he describes were caused by overcrowding from an influx of labourers and poor people, leading to slum conditions and outbreaks of cholera in 1849 and 1854. The conditions are graphically described in the letters of Henry Moule, Vicar of Fordington, to Prince Albert. The overcrowding was in part due to a reluctance by the Duchy of Cornwall, the principal landowner, to enclose the old open fields of Fordington, and release new land for building development. At the other end of the town the plight of the urban poor was made visible for all in the erection of the new Poor Law Union Workhouse on Damers Road. Of this austere cruciform-shaped building, only the east entrance wing now survives, as part of the present Dorset County Hospital. It is thought by some to have been the model for the workhouse in *Far from the Madding Crowd* where Fanny Robin meets her end.

With the enclosure of the Fordington open fields after 1870, Dorchester began to spread rapidly. The progress of development can be followed on the large-scale Ordnance Survey maps of the time. By 1886 Prince of Wales Road had been laid out and villas had appeared along it. There were smaller terraced properties on Great Western Road. Building was well under way on what became known as the Cornwall Estate to the west of the town. Most of the houses were small terraced dwellings, with a few larger terraced houses and villas.

By the time of the 1903 map the Cornwall Estate was complete and the much larger Victoria Park estate to the south-west of the town was being laid out, beginning with Queen's Avenue. This followed the sale in 1896 of 63 acres of building land by the Duchy of Cornwall, the auctioneer commenting on 'the great demand that existed for villa residences'. In fact much of the development in this area was in terraces of working-class housing. Development was slower than the promoters anticipated, with Victoria Park gradually developing throughout the early twentieth century as a self-contained suburb with its own school, post office, church, and shops.

Industrial growth provides one reason why Victorian Dorchester was attracting people looking for work, and for the spread of suburban housing which followed. The opening of the Southampton to Dorchester railway in 1847 and the Great Western line to Yeovil and Westbury ten years later encouraged new commercial enterprises in the town. Foremost among these was the Eldridge Pope brewery opened in 1881, close to the South station and with its own railway siding, and whose chimney, at 125 feet, was 'the loftiest building in the town'. Another venture was the Francis Eddison steam traction engine works, which moved into Fordington from Martinstown. At first the works produced steam plough sets, later moving on to road rollers and traction engines. By 1885 the works was employing 60-70 people, one of the largest employers in the town.

Many of Dorchester's institutions and utilities were remade into a form recognisable to us today. The town acquired its police force in 1836 and its hospital in 1841, described by William Barnes as 'a truly Christian and excellent institution . . . in an open and healthy spot'. The County Museum first opened in 1845 in response to the growing

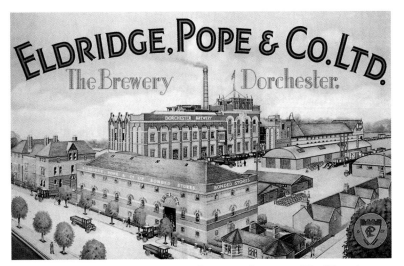

The Eldridge Pope Brewery, Dorchester, in the 1920s. The Victorian brewery complex opened in 1881 and within five years its output had topped 40,000 barrels a year (11½ million pints). The last beer on the site was brewed in 1996 and today the Brewery Square complex is being developed into shops, restaurants, a hotel, apartments and houses.

interest in geological specimens in the area. Public utilities were slower to arrive. The town had gas lighting from 1835 but electricity was long delayed, and it was the early part of the next century before it became more widely available. As early as 1852 the town's Board of Health had recommended a new water and sewage system to replace the contaminated cess pits, but it was another fifty years before the first mains sewage system was operating.

INDUSTRIAL TOWNS
BRIDPORT AND GILLINGHAM

Some towns acquired a distinctly more industrial character. By the eighteenth century Bridport was the principal source of rope, twine and netting in the region. The greater part of the town's population was involved in the manufacture, including many women and children, largely in their own homes. Behind the terraced cottages along South

The old Bridport Net Industries works, St Michael's Lane, Bridport. Even today a walk in the area reveals the remains of an industrial suburb.

Street and parts of East Street, the long medieval burgage plots found a new use as rope spinning walks for the flourishing rope and nets manufacture. Many cottages were rebuilt in the early nineteenth century, often in an individual style, giving variety to today's street frontage. The courts and long gardens extending behind the houses sometimes have brick built sheds and other structures associated with the former industry.

By the early nineteenth century the cottages had largely become the homes of outworkers employed by the steam-powered rope and net factories which were starting to dominate the town. The factories appear to have co-existed with the domestic manufacture rather than superseding it, using the outworkers for the more specialised products. Much of the industry came to be concentrated in the area to the west of South Street and along St. Michael's Lane. A walk along this street shows the remains of an industrial suburb which contained factories, covered rope walks, smaller workshops, and workers' cottages. One of the factory complexes in this area was the Priory Mills, first built by the Whetham company as a steam-powered flax spinning mill in 1838. It was the first to introduce powerlooms to Bridport and the last mill to make sailcloth in the town.

Other factory complexes in Bridport included the Court Mills of the Gundry company, which has been continually in business from the mid-seventeenth century until the present day. The original Court Mills can still be seen fronting on to West Street, but from the mid-nineteenth century the factory buildings were extended to cover a large area to the north, almost all consisting of single and two-storeyed sheds. Other Bridport industries not related to ropes and nets were corn milling, brewing, and tanneries, of which only the Palmers Brewery is still operating.

The industrial growth of Bridport was initially aided by the reconstruction of the harbour, later known as West Bay, by John Rennie in the early 1800s. New streets, workers' housing, and warehouses appeared, some of which can still be seen. A new road gave direct access to Bridport. For a time the harbour had its own customs house and bonded warehouse. Warehousing was used mainly for flax and hemp, and the occupants included the principal Bridport manufacturers. Several of these older buildings remain in the area around George Street. Once the railway reached Bridport the harbour became less essential for the importing of flax and hemp, and turned instead to tourism, a change marked by construction of the distinctive Pier Terrace housing.

Pier Terrace, West Bay, was built at the same time as the railway station. Both were part of an attempted development intended to transform West Bay into a Victorian seaside resort.

Market day in Gillingham near the South-Western Hotel. The town grew following the arrival of the railway in 1859 and the opening of the nearby brickworks.

In the north of the county Gillingham shows how industrial growth followed on from the coming of the railway. The town had long had a silk mill when the arrival of the London and South-Western Railway in 1859 produced new industrial possibilities. The first of these to be realised was the brickworks, created to the south of the town on a site next to the railway, where a huge area of brick clays could now be profitably opened up. Over the next century the distinctive red bricks, tiles, and pottery of the brickfields found their way into new building developments as far afield as the mushrooming area around Bournemouth. The brickworks were soon followed by sawmills, a coal depot, glue factory, livestock market, dairy and milk depots, and bacon factory, defining Gillingham as a processing town for rural produce for much of the next century.

Much of this activity developed some distance away from the older market area around the church. A consequence was a shift in the commercial focus of the town up the High Street towards Newbury and Station Road. High Street was largely rebuilt from the 1860s, with many new shops and services providing an increasing range of goods including manufactured products, hardware, food, clothes, and furniture. Visitors to the town by train could use the Railway Hotel, South-Western Hotel, or the Phoenix, which provided a carriage to meet arriving trains. Buildings such as the Phoenix, and the former Wiltshire and Dorset Bank further up the High Street, are reminders of this period of Gillingham's commercial growth.

OLD PORTS: WEYMOUTH AND POOLE

During the early nineteenth century Weymouth slipped into a period of decadence and stagnation, living off its reputation as a genteel Georgian resort and its royal connection. The decline in visitors may have resulted in part from the appalling sanitary conditions in the town, including open sewers along the main streets and the regular dumping of nightsoil over the quayside. The conditions no doubt contributed to the mortality rate of the town being considerably higher than the national average. While it was claimed that the insanitary areas were 'little known to visitors or the wealthier classes', a local Board of Health, reporting in 1852, recognised the threat to the visitor trade. It tried to set in motion a programme of improvements, but it was to be another forty years before a proper mains drainage scheme was finally put in hand.

The character of the town began to change with events originating from outside its boundary. By the middle of the century Portland was home to a growing number of labourers and convicts, all engaged on the building of the Portland Breakwaters, the Verne Citadel, and the Nothe Fort overlooking Weymouth itself, transforming Portland into a major south coast naval base. The building of the New Breakwater was not completed until 1903, completing Portland's defences. These projects hastened the need for a link to the national railway network, which was opened in 1865.

The following year the first Channel Island packet services began to operate from Weymouth. The Great Western Railway began to lay on extra trains for day trippers, and the future of Weymouth as a major holiday resort was assured. By 1889 trains had direct access to the steamers via a new link running along the harbour wall. The spectacle of trains along the harbourside disappeared with the subsequent reclamation of land from the inlet, but the link itself continued in use until 1984.

Fortuneswell, Portland, 1898. Portland's nineteenth century expansion owed much to the building of the Breakwater and the arrival of the Navy.

From this time Weymouth became less exclusive, attracting many more working people. In contrast to the impressive terraces of the earlier generation, new, smaller rows of houses providing inexpensive lodgings sprang up close to the railway station. Wealthier visitors could avoid them by consulting a 'House and Apartment Register' listing 'better class' accommodation. New streets in the Park district were laid out to a grid-iron plan. The rows were often named as terraces, for example Sydney Terrace or Salisbury Terrace, but the names themselves dropped out of use and were lost when the streets were renumbered early in the next century. Along the Esplanade, now extended northwards, visitors could enjoy the new public walks and gardens given to the town by wealthy residents, such as its Member for Parliament Sir Frederick Johnstone. Another Weymouth MP who gave generously to the town was Sir Henry Edwards, whose statue on the Esplanade is not easily missed; and all visitors to Weymouth would know the Jubilee Clock, erected in 1887 to mark the fiftieth year of Queen Victoria's Reign.

With the collapse of the lucrative Newfoundland trade in the 1820s, Poole entered a period of decline and stagnation, and by 1844 the Poole merchant fleet was only a fifth of its size of thirty years earlier. Throughout this period the town was engulfed in struggles

The 'swivel' bridge between Poole and Hamworthy in 1855. Until the bridge opened in 1837 Hamworthy was reached by ferry.

between its Liberal and Tory politicians, culminating in the bankruptcy of the town council and the seizure of all its property by the High Court. The bar at the harbour entrance restricted the entry of bigger ships, and there was as yet no railway serving the Quay. When the railway did arrive in 1847, initially to Hamworthy, instead of stimulating the economy it brought about a collapse of the coastal trade operating from the quayside. These troubles did not prevent some material progress, much of which was led by its MP William Ponsonby, a champion of reform and improvement. Under his influence Poole became one of the first towns on the south coast to have gas lighting and gained its first bridge, a wooden structure, connecting it with Hamworthy. The bridge served the town until 1885 when it was replaced by an iron one.

Revival came from an unlikely source, the growth of its rival Bournemouth next door along the coast. The boom from the building of the new resort after 1860 produced a surge in the demand for building materials like stone, roofing slates, and timber, which could be imported through Poole. Local clay beds were opened up to provide the raw materials for the thriving brick, tile, drainpipe, and ceramics industries. Several companies flourished, including the Poole Pottery firm of Jesse Carter, which became a leader in artistic ceramics. The

The Hamworthy works of the Patent Architectural Pottery in 1855. The company was the first of the Poole potteries, making mouldings, glazed bricks and ornamental tiles.

town steadily spread out to absorb neighbouring Longfleet, Parkstone, and Hamworthy. The Quay itself was extended out into deeper waters. The amenities of civilised urban life gradually appeared. Parks were laid out, a Public Library, Museum, and School of Art and Science all opened. By 1902 a street tramway linked the town centre to the boundaries of Bournemouth.

THE NEW RESORTS
BOURNEMOUTH, BOSCOMBE, & SWANAGE

The growth of all south coast towns was eclipsed by the speed at which Bournemouth mushroomed from modest beginnings. In 1810 Lewis Tregonwell, attracted by its healthy climate and the pine woodlands, built a holiday home for himself which became known as 'The Mansion', and then a few cottages for servants, friends, and relations. In the 1830s Sir George Tapps-Gervis commissioned

Benjamin Ferrey's design for the Gervis Estate, Bournemouth, in the 1840s. Lewis Tregonwell's holiday home, the first house in Bournemouth, is the large house on the left.

Benjamin Ferrey, a Christchurch architect, to develop a marine 'watering-place' to rival Weymouth and Brighton, leading to the building of Westover Gardens and Villas and the Royal Bath Hotel. A description of the project from 1842 suggested that the new resort had the potential to become 'the very first invalid spa watering place in England . . . a winter residence for the delicate constitutions requiring a warm and sheltered locality'. Sir George was eager to avoid laying out streets of lodging houses and terraces, instead encouraging a unique resort 'for the upper and wealthier classes of society.' However growth was slow and by 1851 there were still only 691 residents. The startling expansion followed after the opening of railway links with London and the Midlands; by 1881 the population had already climbed to over 16,000.

The speed and character of change is well illustrated at the outlying district of Boscombe, a mile or so along the coast, and soon to be absorbed into the growing resort. At the start of the century Boscombe was a common covered with furze and heath, more the haunt of smugglers than anyone else. Substantial development began only in the 1860s when Sir Henry Wolff bought land on which to develop a 'picturesque village of Boscombe Spa'. This was to be based on the

Boscombe Chine Hotel in 1876. The thatched building was known as the Spa and was built over a mineral spring.

springwaters at the mouth of Boscombe Chine, a wooded 'chink' or gap in the coastal cliffs. Various streets for building were laid out, some, like Horace Road, named after members of the Wolff family. The Chine area itself was landscaped and a hotel built, now the Chine Hotel. From these initial developments new estates of villas began to spread out across the heaths and sandy cliffs, so that the magazine *Vanity Fair* referring to Boscombe in 1875, commented: 'separated only by a small ravine from Bournemouth proper is another rising collection of villas . . . Boscombe is a pretty little place somewhat bare at present.'

Boscombe's population increased sixfold in the 1870s, over threefold again in the following decade to 6,324 in 1891, and then to 9,648 in 1901. Developments were carried out by the Boscombe Land Society, which keenly promoted the healthy, wooded character of the area and its suitability for first class villas. The attractions of the town were further enhanced by the opening of the 600 feet long pier in 1889, the pier head having landing stages on each side for excursion steamers. Covered shelters along its length provided ample protection against inclement weather.

Behind the sea frontage the town centre developed, largely the creation of Archibald Beckett. His buildings included the fashionable

Bournemouth's population rose from 405 when Queen Victoria ascended to the throne in 1837 to 65,000 by her death in 1902. Gradually the surrounding heath became satellite townships, as here in this view of the Wimborne Road, Winton, in the early 1900s.

Royal Arcade, which provided not only all-weather shopping lit by electricity, but also entertainments from a stage on the balcony. In 1897 Boscombe gained its own railway station, having previously been served by Pokesdown. The character of Christchurch Road gradually changed as villas gave way to shops. The large and prestigious Burlington Hotel appeared, an Italianate building with 200 bedrooms, thirteen suites of private rooms, a ballroom, and billiards saloon. The whole town was dominated by the massive Chine Hotel, a landmark for Channel shipping and always popular with the leading artists of the variety theatre and music halls, who often used it when appearing in Bournemouth.

Although Boscombe was gradually assimilated into Bournemouth, it remained recognisable as a distinctive resort in its own right. Bournemouth itself continued to spread west across Branksome and Canford, effectively joining it with Poole, and across Southbourne eastwards towards Christchurch. By 1911 it had a population of more than 78,000, by then one of the country's largest towns.

Along the coast, on the eastern end of the Purbeck peninsula, a resort of more modest dimensions was gradually taking shape. In

Swanage and the Bay, from near Peveril Point in 1823, the year the young
Princess Victoria stayed in the town.

previous centuries Swanage had been little more than a fishing village
and slipway for the shipping of Purbeck stone. One description of
inhabitants described them as '. . . something exceptionally primitive
. . . chiefly quarrymen, and like all quarry folk . . . a strangely reserved
and isolated race.'

William Morton Pitt of Kingston Maurward and a Dorset MP,
considered that the village had more potential than as a place for the
export of stone, envisaging a watering place to rival Weymouth and
Lyme Regis. He converted the old manor house into a hotel, which
became known as the Royal Victoria Hotel following a visit by the
young Princess Victoria in 1833. The town remained limited to a few
terraces until the building of the pier for pleasure steamers began to
attract more people, who at this time were still of a professional and
middle class character.

One visitor who came to stay was John Mowlem, a local Swanage
man, returning from making his fortune in London. Along with his
nephew and partner, John Burt, he set out to improve the town. He
built the Mowlem Institute as a reading room 'for the benefit and
mutual improvement of the working classes', now replaced by a
modern building, and in 1863 erected the Alfred Monument to
celebrate Alfred's supposed victory over the Danes in Swanage Bay.
Burt built the Town Hall, which incorporates a frontage from Mercer's
hall, Cheapside, which he dismantled and brought to Swanage.

The coming of the railway in 1881 led to further growth as the resort began to attract a wider public. A diary of the Thurston family, who stayed at Swanage for six weeks in 1874, gives a flavour of the resort. They stayed at a house in Exeter Place where they had two sitting rooms and two bedrooms for 3½ guineas a week. The diary tells us 'Swanage was a place where you can do as one likes, as there is no promenade to make a small appearance at and where one can escape from the gaze of human beings.' Pre-railway Swanage was 'not infested so much with visitors as other places are . . . Swanage is an admirable place for walking, boating, excursions, and every other amusement.'

TURN OF THE CENTURY

By the first decade of the twentieth century all of Dorset's towns were recognisably different from how they had been at the start of Victoria's reign. Picture postcards of this period show how the rebuilding of houses and public buildings using brick, stone, and slate, had significantly altered the appearance of streets. These in turn were properly paved, surfaced, and lit. Residents could feel secure knowing that local police and fire stations were nearby, and hoped that the gradual appearance of local hospitals might extend their lives. The nearby railway station had made it relatively inexpensive to travel, and also brought a wider range of goods into their high street shops.

There were some towns which otherwise had changed little from a century earlier. At Beaminster, Sturminster Newton, Sherborne, or Cerne Abbas, the layout of streets and the general extent of the town would have been entirely familiar to early generations. By contrast at Poole, Weymouth, and Dorchester the old town, while recognisable as a distinctive area, was becoming absorbed into a wider spread of streets and suburbs based on the commercial successes of the railway age. The explosive growth of Bournemouth was unmatched anywhere else on the south coast. In the next century the motor age was to bring far-reaching changes to all towns, large and small.

THE MODERN AGE

The first half of the twentieth century was a period of contradiction, of both stability and change. Soldiers returning home in 1945 found towns which at first sight were little different from those which their predecessors had left to fight the first war in 1914. Many of the older, smaller towns had hardly grown, or even declined in population. There were few new streets, and most buildings had been built prior to 1914.

Only on closer inspection were the differences apparent, most noticeably in the dominance of the motor vehicle and the virtual disappearance of horse-drawn traffic. Dusty streets were giving way to hard, tarmacadam surfaces. There were a lot more traffic signs and street lights, while garages and the workshops of motor engineers were widely in evidence. Overhead, telegraph poles and cables heralded the new age of mass communication; while within people's homes the wireless had finally ended the isolation of the rural town from the world outside.

Between the two wars, the older market towns seemed timeless, little changed for generations. The streets of Blandford Forum on market days in 1920 were crowded with villagers from the Winterborne and Tarrant valleys. Conversations in the pubs and on street corners were all about crops, animals, and farm prices. Blandford however differed from some other towns because of its dependence on the nearby mansion and estate at Bryanston. Every morning scores of people crossed the bridge over the Stour and walked up the long driveway to work in the house, kitchens, and grounds of the estate of Lord Portman. Blandford shops relied heavily on sales of food and everyday goods to the Bryanston Estate. What must have seemed like an unchanging order of things came to an end in the mid 1920s when the estate was sold to pay death duties, and the livelihoods of much of the population were suddenly put in doubt. But by this time Blandford

The Market Place, Blandford, in the late 1920s. The small crowd is gathered round a stallholder selling household utensils.

was experiencing prosperity from a different source. In the First World War a new camp was hurriedly built on nearby Monkton Down, soon becoming a permanent feature of the landscape. The town filled with troops. Once stagnating shops and services rapidly expanded, and Blandford acquired a further role as a military town, one which it still has at the present day.

Shaftesbury also entered a new era at this time. In 1919 Lord Stalbridge, owner of much of the town, auctioned it off in 300 lots. Most tenants were able to buy their own premises, the sale including shops, houses, and inns. The Corporation bought the fire station, market house, and cattle market. The Park and Castle Hill were given as open spaces. The following years saw the town move into a more modern age with an extension of municipal involvement, including the advent of cemeteries, council houses, and electric street lighting. The fire brigade took possession of their first motorised fire engine. Mains water and sewerage were extended. The first refuse disposal collection was instituted. Residents witnessed their streets gradually being taken over by the motor vehicle, helped by the growth of motoring in the 1920s and the town's position as a stopping point on the road from London to the south-west. Some traditions endured. In 1920 the watchmaker George Hillier was appointed 'winder of clocks at the Town Hall and curfew bell ringer,' a service which continued until after the Second World War.

Dorchester suffered grievously in the First World War, losing 237 men from a population of nine thousand. Some shops displayed a sign 'Closed till the end of the war', and a handful never reopened. Returning soldiers noticed a subdued, quieter, town, with streets deserted for longer periods and shops closing earlier in the evening; a contrast to the Edwardian town, when commercial life had extended to the very end of the day. Under the influence of the growing interest in Thomas Hardy, Dorchester was already acquiring a reputation as a quaint, nostalgic place, the focus of a backward rural county, and seemed destined to remain by-passed by newer developments.

Yet even Dorchester was not immune to change. In 1923 the Borough was granted the right to widen the Top of Town because of the increase in motor traffic. Another equally visible symbol of the modern age was the arrival of the Marconi Beam Wireless Station, one of only two transmitters in the country for beam wireless, with masts 227 feet high. In 1926 an Electrical Exhibition at the Corn Exchange included washing machines and vacuum cleaners. By the 1930s there

High West Street, Dorchester, in 1920.
Note the garage on the left hand side.

Cheap Street, Sherborne, in the 1920s, the brief period when both horse-drawn traffic and the motor car shared Dorset's high streets.

were cinemas in Durngate Street and Trinity Street. Despite the depression, new shops appeared, a notable addition being the art deco building of Thurmans in South Street. By 1937, 172 council houses had been been built. The extension of local government into the lives of Dorset people was symbolised in the purchase by the County Council of Colliton House and its grounds, to become the new County Hall. This building project was started in 1938 but was delayed by the war, and not completed until 1955.

It was in the south of the county that urban growth took on a more sustained form. In Weymouth by the 1930s new housing developments had started to advance up the western side of Radipole Lake, including many of the 500 council houses to be built in the town by the 1950s. The boundaries of Weymouth were extended in 1933 to include Broadwey, Upwey, Preston, Radipole, and Wyke Regis, giving the borough a population of 37,000 by 1951.

Nothing describes the impact of the motor car on Dorset's towns better than this aerial view of Charles Trent's car scrapyard at Newtown in the 1930s. This whole area of Poole has since been developed.

Further eastwards Bournemouth continued the rapid rate of expansion started in the previous century, swallowing up Boscombe, Westbourne, and Southbourne. Soon it was barely separate from Parkstone and Poole. North of the town new middle-class suburbs were established at Talbot Woods, Ensbury Park, and Richmond Park, confirming Bournemouth as one of the most popular towns in the south of England.

Poole experienced comparable growth, reaching 57,200 by 1931. By this time it had expanded well north of the railway to absorb the urban district of Branksome and the rural district of Canford Magna. Suburban development was starting to eat into the great expanse of Canford Heath which had previously stretched uninterruptedly from Parkstone to Wimborne. The major employers of the town were its gas company, boatbuilding (particularly of yachts), and its brickyards and potteries. The Poole Pottery company especially flourished, becoming well known for its vivid hand-painted designs. New municipal buildings appeared in 1932, and the town, having been one of the first to adopt electric trams, saw its last tram run in 1935. The harbour became attractive to painters and artists, including Augustus John, Henry Lamb, Bernard Gribble, and others who depicted scenes of its old streets and harbour.

The Second World War ushered in a new, albeit temporary phase to the appearance and character of Dorset's coastal towns. The entire sea frontage of Bournemouth and Poole became a fortified zone, with all beaches mined and strewn with barbed wire and concrete obstacles. Poole itself rapidly changed from an artists' haven to a war zone, its streets littered with air-raid shelters and water tanks, and the town itself surrounded by a cordon of concrete 'dragon's teeth.' Air raids brought damage to some 5,000 homes. Bournemouth became a reception area for evacuees from Southampton, Portsmouth and London, and also home to some government departments. Bombing raids in 1943 destroyed several hotels and department stores. Weymouth was a major loading port for the invasion of Normandy, seeing half a million troops and over 140,000 vehicles embarked between June 1944 and May 1945.

SINCE 1945

The early post-war years brought little immediate change to Dorset's towns. This was a period of economic hardship, with hardly any money available for rebuilding or new developments. Poole began the post-war era with a backlog of 700 houses in the Old Town condemned as slums prior to the war but still in use. Many streets were without made-up roads, lights, and drainage. Its parks and open spaces had been dug up for wartime food production. The grim realities of post-war austerity were brought home by the closure of the BOAC seaplane base and the loss of 600 jobs. Government limits on spending meant delays in the programmes of slum clearance and council house rebuilding. It was not until the early 1960s that the council house waiting list was substantially eliminated, mostly through the construction of tower blocks and maisonettes.

By this time Poole was changing in other ways and beginning to resemble the town of today. A new road system linked the eastern and western sides of the town for the first time and gave incoming traffic better access to Poole Bridge and the harbour area. A new bridge over the railway overcame the town's access problems via the existing level crossings. In the 1960s the Arndale Centre shopping development included the first Sainsbury supermarket to desert a traditional 'high street' location for a covered precinct. In 1976 the opening of Barclay House on its island site, 145 high and with 1600 parking spaces, seemed to herald the dawn of a new, more prosperous age. At the same time as the new Poole took shape, an awareness of the town's past was causing a growing minority to fight proposals to demolish the historic areas of the Old Town, leading to its designation as a conservation area and ultimate recognition of its heritage importance.

Since the 1960s all Dorset towns have experienced a revival in population growth. Gillingham, with a population of 3,350 in 1951, had reached double that size by 1991 and has since continued to grow to reach almost three times the 1951 figure by 2001. Wareham doubled its population over the same half-century, largely due to the Northport developments across the river outside the old town; and Wimborne increased by half its 1951 size over the same half-century. In the south of the county population growth and urban expansion has generated entirely new urban entities. In 1974 Bournemouth was added to Dorset, and in 1997 Poole and Bournemouth became a single unitary authority with a combined population of 301,000. The boundaries of this new unit extended northwards from the coast to the River Stour and the boundaries of Wimborne. By this date it included large new developments at Corfe Mullen, Merley, and Broadstone, all of which half a century earlier had been largely open countryside. The only extensive open land remaining was Canford Heath, itself a fragment of the far bigger heathland of earlier decades. Across the Stour Wimborne had spawned a new suburb at Colehill, and there were new urban areas at Ferndown, West Moors, Ashley Heath, and Verwood.

Broadstone owed its early growth to its location on the Somerset and Dorset Railway, and began to grow as a sizeable community during the 1960s, precisely at the time when the railway was closed.

Slums in the Old Town, Poole. Blue Boar Lane in 1957.

It is now an outlying residential district of Poole, but maintains a strong sense of identity. Ferndown in the 1950s had been a sizeable village strung out along the main roads to Poole and Wimborne and some neighbouring side roads, and was well known to passing motorists and Bournemouth holidaymakers for its zoo. New housing developments at Trickett's Cross began its transformation into a small town; by 1977 it had its own town council, and by 1985 it had gained the by-pass which now defines its northern boundary. To the south Ferndown has merged with West Parley, which is separated from Bournemouth only by a mile of green belt land on the flood plain of the Stour. Verwood, now with a population of 13,000, originally developed through its distinctive pottery industry, but much employment is now provided by its industrial estate.

One force behind the new urban growth has been the movement of modern, light industries into the region, attracted by a developing road network, nearness to the port of Poole, space for industrial estates and business parks, and a high quality of environment. The 1980s saw a steady movement of financial services into the Bournemouth and Poole area, with a spread of business parks and office developments, all bringing new jobs and stimulating the need for more housing. Another factor has been the development of tourism outside the traditional Bournemouth holiday area, together with the growing interest in the county's heritage. This has particularly benefited Dorchester with its Thomas Hardy associations, prehistoric and Roman remains, closeness to the 'Jurassic' coast, and central position within the county, but other towns such as Wareham, Bridport, and Sherborne have also shared in the visitor influx.

In recent years lifestyle considerations have led to a growing number of people moving into the county eager to savour all Dorset has to offer, especially for retirement and second home ownership. Along the coast old harbours and quaysides have been transformed into sailing clubs and marinas flanked by newly built properties. In some towns the 'retired' element of the population is now more than 60% of the total, and well above the county average. One result has been a steady rise in property prices in many towns, most marked in the area around Poole and Sandbanks, which now includes some of the most expensive real estate in the country. Some places have also attracted people through their lively arts scenes, such as at Poole and Bridport. The Poole Arts centre was refurbished in the 1990s and reopened as The Lighthouse, a landmark building which is also a focus for the arts in Poole. The Bridport Arts Centre includes a theatre, art workshops and galleries, giving the town an importance as an arts centre beyond what might be expected for its size. The Arts Centre in Shaftesbury and the reopened Tivoli Theatre in Wimborne also attract wide followings.

CHANGING TOWNSCAPES

Many towns now have little to show of their former industrial and commercial importance, or of their former links with the surrounding countryside. Their markets and agriculturally-based industries have disappeared, along with the buildings and structures associated with them.

Gillingham's example is fairly typical. Its brickyard, livestock market, and most of its food manufacturing had disappeared by 1970, only the bacon factory remaining until 1985. Redundant buildings have been demolished to make way for a business park, industrial estate, and space for the town centre by-pass. The most prominent building, the town mills, was destroyed by fire and a block of flats now stands in its place.

At Sturminster Newton the livestock market, which had been the focus of the town's trade for generations, ceased trading in 1997 when the market site was sold. Shortly afterwards the cheese factory and cattle breeding unit also closed, bringing to an end the town's long history as agricultural capital of the Blackmore Vale. It is only most recently, with the redevelopment of the old market site, that the town has found an opportunity to move forward.

In Bridport, by contrast, much more remains of the commercial heritage. Many of the mills and warehouses once used by the rope and nets industries still survive. Some are occupied by the newer, smaller businesses which have set up in the town in recent years, but others have been partially disused or derelict for a long time. There is a particular concentration of these buildings to the south-west of the town centre, an area which is now becoming widely recognised for its importance as one of the earliest known industrial suburbs in the country. Other early industrial buildings in Bridport include West Mill and Palmer's Brewery, still very much at work. The Victorian and older streets have been largely unchanged by modern development, so that the town remains relatively well endowed with remains from the past.

In and around Bournemouth, modern development and redevelopment is more in evidence, often side by side with the Victorian past. In the 1960s the resort still exerted much of its traditional charm. 'It was still very genteel even though there were holidaymakers, and you could still hire a bath chair for the afternoon and some one to push it,' wrote one entertainer who performed regularly at the resort. 'The holidaymakers were very upper crust and all took dinner at their hotels.' Bournemouth during the day was very much about its beaches, gardens, high class shops and department stores, while the evening entertainments revolved around the Winter Gardens and the Pavilion Theatre. Like all resorts, Bournemouth has had to find a new way forward. Representative of a new image is the Bournemouth International Centre, which recently underwent a major refurbishment programme, making it a nationally leading venue for conferences, exhibitions, and top entertainment attractions.

Dorset's towns have largely escaped the wholesale redevelopments which transformed towns elsewhere in the 1960s and 1970s. In some cases the need for modern amenities has been met by integrating new functions and uses into older buildings. In Dorchester the open spaces and large gardens which once lay behind the fashionable properties of the main streets have given way to new development, but the outbuildings and stables remain, often converted into shops and offices. In Cornhill the frontage of the Antelope Hotel has been retained to give access to the shopping arcade which lies behind; in South Street the Napper's Mite almshouse frontage conceals a restaurant with further shops behind; and the former County Hospital and Fordington foundry keep their original appearances but have taken on new residential functions. In Shaftesbury the site of the old Swan Inn has been used to create a pedestrian thoroughfare between two main streets, with new shops and craft outlets; on the wall of the new Swan's Yard a mural in the form of a window invites you to look through the frame towards the recreation of a market scene of the seventeenth century.

The fast-growing 'urban village' of Poundbury to the west of Dorchester is often cited as a blueprint for towns and villages in the new century. The project is unique in being the outcome not of planners' deliberations but of the inspiration of one person, the Prince of Wales. The objective is to develop a new sort of country village or town, no longer based on farming or markets as in the past, but using the best ideas from older towns in a modern context. The target is for 2,400 homes on 53 hectares of land to be completed by 2025, increasing the population of Dorchester by 5,000. The innovative, pioneering ideas include the mix of higher income and 'social' housing within one community; the dispersal of commercial functions close to where people live, not in separate business parks; the attention given

A view of Poundbury in the summer of 2008. When finished, the 'urban
village' will consist of 2,400 homes, as well as offices, shops,
a market hall, and other amenities.

to architectural detail; the encouragement given to keep vehicle
parking off the streets; and the incorporation of 'green' and energy-
saving features in the design.

The types of houses include a range of traditional Dorset architectural
materials and styles. Bricks are laid in Flemish Bond, brick is banded
with flint, while stonework is sometimes arranged in random courses
and elsewhere as carefully dressed ashlar blocks. Traditional casement
windows look across the street at Victorian sash windows, recreating
the contrast between the Georgian and Victorian houses which
dominate Dorset towns and villages. The development has a main
square overlooked by an open market hall with columns and steeply
pitched roof, and home to regular farmers' markets.

Future generations will judge the success of Poundbury. It has its
detractors, who see it as little more than a pastiche of past styles
destined to become just another suburb of Dorchester. Others applaud
its distinctive features and point to its continuing success in attracting
new residents. Houses and layouts of similar look are making an
appearance in neighbouring towns and villages. Whatever its future, it
is already adding a new chapter to the story of Dorset's towns.

FURTHER READING

A starting point for the study of towns anywhere in Britain is David Lloyd's *The Making of English Towns* (1984). There are introductions to the history of the Wessex region generally in Barry Cunliffe's *Wessex to AD 1000* (1993) and Joe Bettey's *Wessex from AD 1000* (1986), both of which place the growth of Dorset's towns in the wider regional context. The Roman period is fully described in Bill Putnam's Roman Dorset (2007).

Town development is a theme which occurs frequently in several of the books of the 'Discover Dorset' series of Dovecote Press, especially the volumes on *Tudors and Stuarts* By Joe Bettey (2006), *The Georgians* (Jo Draper, 1998), *Regency, Riot, and Reform* (Jo Draper, 2000), and *The Victorians* (Jude James, 1998), all of which are well illustrated with period pictures and have good references to further reading.

Most of Dorset's towns have recent books outlining their historical development. These include:

Attwooll, M. and West J., *Weymouth, An Illustrated History.* 1995
Cullingford C.N., *A History of Poole.* 1988
Draper J., *Dorchester, An Illustrated History.* 1992
Edwards E., *A History of Bournemouth.* 1981
Eedle, M de G., *A History of Beaminster.* 1984
Hillier J., *Victorian Poole.* 1990
Howe, C., *Gylla's Hometown.* 1983
Innes B, *Shaftesbury, An Illustrated History.* 1992
James J, *Wimborne Minster: The History of a Country Town.* 1992
Lewer D. and Smale D., *Swanage Past.* 1994.

The expanding series of *Halsgove Community Histories* includes volumes on Beaminster, Blandford, Bridport, Cerne Abbas, and Lyme Regis, all with much period illustration.

Recent archaeological and historical research on Dorset's towns is covered in the *Proceedings* of the Dorset Natural History and Archaeological Society and in the *Somerset and Dorset Notes and Queries*. The former has particularly interesting items of recent work on Shaftesbury (Vol.125 and 122), Gillingham (123), Bridport (122), Lyme Regis (120), and Dorchester (117).

A starting point for architectural studies in Dorset's towns is the four volumes of the *Inventory of Historical Monuments in the County of Dorset*, published by Royal Commission in 1970.

All of Dorset's historians owe a debt to John Hutchins and his *History of Dorset*, first published in 1774 and enlarged to four volumes in 1861-70.

In recent years the internet has started to become an indispensable historical source. The website of the *Images of England* project by English Heritage (www.imagesofengland.org.uk) can provide architectural detail for many of the listed buildings in Dorset's towns.

ACKNOWLEDGEMENTS

I should like to thank David Burnett for his careful reading of the text and invaluable suggestions for improvements. The collections of the Dorset History Centre have been a constant source for reference and research. Further thanks are owed to my wife Margaret for her proof reading and compilation of the index.

Most of the illustrations are taken from the Collection of the Dovecote Press, but I am grateful to the following for allowing the use of illustrations in their possession or for which they hold the copyright: Adrian Cooper, pages 2, 8, 22 (top left and top right), 25 (top right), 26, 27 (both), 28, 30, 40, 50 (both), 54, 57, 60, 61, 83; Gillingham Museum, page 62; Red House Museum, Christchurch, page 12. The map on page 6 was drawn by Christopher Chaplin.

INDEX

The

DISCOVER DORSET

Series of Books

A series of paperback books providing informative illustrated
introductions to Dorset's history, culture and way of life.
The following titles have so far been published.

BLACKMORE VALE *Hilary Townsend*
BRIDGES *David McFetrich and Jo Parsons*
CASTLES AND FORTS *Colin Pomeroy*   COAST & SEA *Sarah Welton*
CRANBORNE CHASE *Desmond Hawkins*
DOWNS, MEADOWS & PASTURES *Jim White*
DRESS AND TEXTILES *Rachel Worth*   FARMING *J.H. Bettey*
FARMHOUSES & COTTAGES *Michael Billett*
FOLLIES *Jonathan Holt*   FOSSILS *Richard Edmonds*
GEOLOGY *Paul Ensom*   THE GEORGIANS *Jo Draper*
HEATHLANDS *Lesley Haskins*   THE INDUSTRIAL PAST *Peter Stanier*
ISLE OF PURBECK *Paul Hyland*   LEGENDS *Jeremy Harte*
LOST VILLAGES *Linda Viner*   MILLS *Peter Stanier*
PLACE-NAMES *A.D. Mills*   PORTLAND *Stuart Morris*
POTTERY *Penny Copland-Griffiths*   THE PREHISTORIC AGE *Bill Putnam*
RAILWAY STATIONS *Mike Oakley*   REGENCY, RIOT & REFORM *Jo Draper*
RIVERS & STREAMS *John Wright*
ROADS, TRACKS & TURNPIKES *David Viner*
THE ROMANS *Bill Putnam*   SAXONS & VIKINGS *David Hinton*
SHIPWRECKS *Maureen Attwooll*   STONE QUARRYING *Jo Thomas*
TOWNS *John Porter*   TUDORS & STUARTS *J.H. Bettey*
THE VICTORIANS *Jude James*   WOODLANDS *Anne Horsfall*

All the books about Dorset published by The Dovecote Press
are available in bookshops throughout the county,
or in case of difficulty direct from the publishers.
The Dovecote Press Ltd, Stanbridge, Wimborne Minster, Dorset BH21 4JD
Tel: 01258 840549 www.dovecotepress.com